One Thing I Know

To order additional copies of *One Thing I Know,* by James Coffin, call 1-800-765-6955.

Visit us at www.reviewandherald.com for information on other Review and Herald® products.

One Thing I Know

(and Other Stuff I Strongly Suspect)

JAMES COFFIN

REVIEW AND HERALD® PUBLISHING ASSOCIATION
HAGERSTOWN, MD 21740

The author assumes full responsibility for the accuracy of all facts and quotations as cited in this book.

This book was
Edited by Lori Peckham
Copyedited by James Cavil
Cover designed by Bond Design
Typeset: 11/14 Bembo

PRINTED IN U.S.A.

07 06 05 04 03 5 4 3 2 1

R&H Cataloging Service
Coffin, James Nathan, 1951-
One thing I know (and other stuff I strongly suspect)

1. Christian life. 2. Spiritual life. 3. Religious life. I. Title.

248.4

ISBN 0-8280-1759-X

Dedication

This book is dedicated to Leonie—my wife,
my lover, my best friend,
and the one who has most inspired me
to be less judgmental, less legalistic,
and less willing to settle for religious clichés and platitudes.

Special thanks to

Penny Shell, who as guidance counselor during my senior year (1969-1970) at Sunnydale Academy in Missouri, pressured me to enter a script-writing contest that, when I won, convinced me that maybe writing could be fun.

Newbold College, whose lecturers impressed upon me the importance of clear thinking and clear expression.

Insight, for printing my first published article.

William G. Johnsson, for hiring me as an assistant editor of the *Adventist Review,* introducing me to writing from the editorial perspective.

Jocelyn Fay and Aileen Sox, fellow editors at the *Adventist Review,* for teaching me the nuts and bolts of writing and editing.

Gary Krause and Bruce Manners, my associate editors at Signs Publishing Company in Australia, for polishing most of the material in this book when it was initially published as editorials.

Karen Gardner, office administrator of Markham Woods church, for proofreading the book manuscript.

Jeannette Johnson, acquisitions editor of the Review and Herald Publishing Association, for being so nice to work with.

Lori Peckham, for editing so well and tuning in to my writing style so completely that any changes are how I wish I'd written it originally.

Contents

MUSINGS AND OBSERVATIONS

FACTS AND FABLES

SCRIPTURE RECONSIDERED

MUSINGS AND OBSERVATIONS

Feeding the Pigeons

A few years ago when I was working in a large city, I'd take a walk each day during my lunch break. My route often took me past an old warehouse, which I assumed stored grain.

Nearly every day grain was strewn over the pavement outside the warehouse. *They must be pretty sloppy in unloading it,* I mused. *But at least it makes the pigeons happy.*

Yet as I saw the grain scattered there day after day I began to wonder if indeed it had been spilled. The warehouse seemed abandoned, so it was hard to imagine trucks dropping grain there so frequently.

Three or four months passed before the mystery was solved. One day I rounded the corner in time to see a frail old man walking across the street with a large bag of grain over his shoulder. It was all he could do to carry it.

As I watched, he untied the bag and began scattering the contents onto the pavement. Pigeons appeared from everywhere. When the bag was empty, he walked back across the street to an old pickup, which I saw was loaded with more bags of grain.

"Do you feed these birds every day?" I asked, approaching him.

"I sure do," he said. "And I feed the ducks down in the park during the winter—when everyone stays at home and doesn't give a thought about what the ducks are going to eat. The authorities never seem to do it, you know."

"But doesn't it cost you a lot?"

"You want to know the truth? It costs my whole Social Security check. If I didn't have a little money coming in from the apartment I rent out, I couldn't do it. But I don't mind. I've made this my little project to make the world a better place."

Before long this man and I seemed to meet regularly (I think he might have adjusted his schedule to correspond with mine). When we spoke, he often shared a bit of his homespun philosophy.

Friends, politicians, preachers—they had all disappointed him, he said. But pigeons and ducks—they had never let him down.

In fact, during the Depression, when his mother couldn't find food for the table, pigeons had become his family's mainstay, thanks to his .22 rifle. And the occasional duck—which strongly resembled those that roamed in the city park—had somehow found its way into his mother's oven.

He reckoned he wasn't exaggerating when he said that he owed his life to those birds. So the least he could do was show them a bit of appreciation now.

His little project to make the world a better place.

The man was eccentric. No doubt about it. But I like eccentrics. They're more interesting than run-of-the-mill people who take walks around the block during their lunch breaks to clear their head of cobwebs.

Eccentrics don't need to race with the pack. And were it not for them, we'd probably never be forced to question why we do some of the things we do.

Not many months later, I moved on. I haven't seen the old man since, and I don't know if he's still feeding the pigeons. But I do know that some of his homespun philosophy has stuck with me. In fact, it has grown on me with time.

Since meeting that old man, I've often asked myself just what I'm doing—or not doing—to make the world a better place.

Do I make sure that I keep in touch with the old widow down the street who has no relatives? Do I volunteer a few hours at the local hospital? Am I helping some under-privileged child learn to read?

Do I contribute to the Humane Society? Do I care for the plants at the church? Do I make sure that I always set aside a certain amount of time each day for my children? Do I regularly wash the dishes? Do I have any little project to make the world a better place?

I think the old man may have been onto something. He was a pretty astute fellow—more astute than he let on, I think. In fact, just the other day I was thinking about him when a radical thought struck me.

What if that old man had actually planned it all? What if he knew all along that people would stop and ask him questions? What if he knew they'd stay to listen to what he had to say, and then go away and think about it? What if he knew that they might do something about it? What if his "little project to make the world a better place" really had little to do with feeding pigeons and ducks?

MUSINGS AND OBSERVATIONS

Goat Tales

Solomon said that we can become wise by observing ants. Jesus said that lilies reveal crucial truths. But a goat taught me one of life's most important lessons: that it takes only a moment to destroy a friendship forever.

When I was a youngster, my sisters and I raised a goat kid on a bottle. We dubbed him "Billy," and it didn't take long for him to reveal his prowess as an escape artist.

No fence on the farm could hold him. The slightest flaw in woven wire seemed to beckon him like a siren's song. Every angled corner brace was a ladder just waiting to be climbed. Any farm implement left too near a barrier provided a launchpad to adventure.

Billy's name was soon upgraded to "William the Conqueror," because he could indeed conquer every device designed to prevent his exits and entrances.

With his goat-green eyes, he would study our every move as we opened grain-bin doors or gates. He would slowly turn his head from side to side as he watched, as if calculating just how he was going to translate our hand action to his mouth action. Few fasteners of human design were Billy-proof.

Undeniably, Billy was the king of nuisances—but such a friendly nuisance! He loved human company and would follow my father around the barnyard like a puppy dog—if he hadn't already escaped from the barnyard, that is.

So how did Billy teach me a lesson?

We had set up an electric cattle fence to keep our cows in a specific section of the pasture. However, the fence was somehow shorting out, and my father was having difficulty finding the problem.

To determine if current was going through the wire, my father would touch the wire with a weed. The limited conductivity of the weed meant that he would get just enough shock to let him know if the fence was working. Rather than pull a new weed each time he tested the fence on one particular day, he just left a weed hanging on it.

As fate would have it, Billy was on the prowl that morning. When he spied a tasty-looking piece of greenery that seemed to be there for the taking, he didn't need an invitation. My father stepped out of the barn just in time to see Billy take the entire weed into his mouth.

At this point I should explain two things: First, the fence operated on a pulsating current. So Billy was able to get a solid bite on the weed before the electricity hit. Second, a weed's conductivity is substantially greater in a wet mouth than in a dry hand—a truth that hit Billy hard, whether he comprehended the finer details or not.

When the electricity zapped him, Billy let out a sound that only an electrocuted goat can emit. He released his hold on the weed and sprang back from the fence. It was a totally new experience, and he didn't desire an encore. However, the scene was so comical that my father let out a belly laugh. And at the sound, the stunned goat turned and looked at him.

Now, I don't know what thought forms go through a goat's mind at such times. But here was a human, a man he had trusted, who obviously was finding immense pleasure in the greatest pain he had ever felt.

And the friendship ended in that instant, never to be revived. The distrust never diminished during the remaining six or seven years of Billy's life.

Billy didn't discount the entire human race—just the man who had laughed at him when he most needed support and comfort. Billy would follow my mother, my sisters, or me as lovingly as ever. But let my father appear, and Billy beat a hasty retreat.

It's a lesson worth pondering: Friendships can take a long time to build. But one ill-advised action can destroy a friendship in a moment.

Billy taught me that lesson well.

MUSINGS AND OBSERVATIONS

Great Teacher, Great Deceiver

No comforter is so effective as the one who has passed through fires of affliction similar to those that the sufferer is trying to cope with. People who've had children, for instance, usually are more understanding than nonparents when they see a harried mother or father trying to cope with energetic, inquisitive children while sitting in church, or shopping.

In developing sensitivity, providing insight, and creating balance, experience is a teacher without a peer. The crucial question is whether the student has come to grips with the entire lesson or has absorbed only scattered fragments. "A little learning is a dangerous thing," whatever the source of knowledge. While experience may produce positive results, it's equally capable of making one insensitive and narrow-minded.

Few are so callous as those who *feel* that they've passed through the sufferer's experience, coped with it easily, and are certain that everyone else should be capable of the same.

If through sound child-rearing practices or genetic fluke (they invariably maintain it's the former) parents have had children who sit placidly with folded hands, learn to whisper before learning to shout, and never speak with a mouthful of food, these parents may find any lesser behavior despicable. Such people *know from experience* that perfect parenting guarantees a perfect product (despite the fact that the first three chapters of the Bible invalidate their position).

Experience-engendered intolerance is widespread. "I've met [x number of] people from [such and such a background]. Every one of them was lazy, dishonest, stupid; therefore, *I know* . . ." Or "I've traveled through [blank country]—spent two whole days there—so you can't tell me . . ."

The person who was receptive immediately to the truths of Adventism may judge as insincere those for whom conviction comes more slowly. The person who never has been attracted to a certain type of sin may view someone who is attracted as degenerate. The highly educated or wealthy may be incapable of appreciating the perspectives of the average person—and the reverse phenomenon is equally true.

Because a person behaved in a certain way at some time in the past doesn't mean that such a person will never change. Time passes. New factors are introduced. People mature. The Holy Spirit guides.

So I'm not denying the inestimable value of experience. I'm simply suggesting that experiential knowledge, like theoretical knowledge, is often limited. It's often a partial truth rather than a universal truth. And it can leave us in danger of being misguided.

What has potential to be a great teacher can in fact become a great deceiver.

Guilty

Today I stand condemned. Guilty. Shamed.

Oh, I haven't committed some heinous crime that will make me detestable in the eyes of the public. In fact, if I weren't telling you, no one would know.

But deep inside I know I'm guilty of treating another human being with indifference. I've been callous.

When I moved to my present location, I couldn't help immediately noticing a certain young man. He was an avid walker, and I supposed he lived somewhere near me. I noticed him not merely because I so often saw him walking along the footpaths and streets, but because of the way he walked.

I would guess that he was in his early 20s. He held his left arm in a manner to suggest that it was of little use. His left leg seemed shorter than his right, and he dragged it somewhat with each step. Walking seemed difficult for him. Yet he regularly made his laborious way from one end of the community to the other.

He never seemed to speak—not that I ever spoke to him, of course. And I judged from his bodily movements and the look in his eye that he'd just as soon be left alone. Besides, his appearance suggested that he and I were . . . well, not on the same wavelength.

Frequently he wore movie-star-style reflective sunglasses. And in warm weather he often wore no shirt, leaving to view tattoos covering his back and upper arms.

For two and a half years he has trudged past. For two and a half years my eyes have been cast down whenever we've met on the foot-path—lest they meet his, and I do not know how to respond.

But that all changed today.

Today I was taking the kids down to the river for a splash. There he was standing by the road thumbing a ride. *Why not?* I thought. *Why not pick him up?*

I'd never seen his tattoos so close-up before. He was wearing no shirt, of course.

When I asked where he was going, he pointed to his mouth and shook his head. As I'd suspected, he was mute. But not deaf.

With his right hand he reached across to his left hip pocket and took out a notepad. He wrote out the details of his destination. Then he got in the car, and as I drove, he went on to converse about other things. He wrote; I spoke.

"Are you here just for the day?" he asked.

"No, I live here. On Salisbury Avenue."

He seemed to suddenly lose all reserve. "I don't remember seeing you before. How long have you lived here, if I may ask?"

The "if I may ask" seemed to be going far beyond the call of duty—at least for a person who had to write every word on a notepad held by an unwieldy left hand.

"I've just shaved off my beard, so I don't look like I used to." I was glad he didn't associate me with the person who always passed him with eyes cast down.

The conversation continued. I'd never realized how much personality could be projected through a few words on a notepad. He wasn't the standoffish, leave-me-to-myself type of person I'd picked him to be. He was warm and gracious. He took a personal interest in me. He asked questions about *me*.

With a sweep of the hand and a point of the finger he indicated that we'd arrived at his destination. But he paused to write another message before getting out: "Thanks for the ride. It was nice meeting you. Have a happy year." He then shook my hand warmly and dragged himself out the door to his feet.

I watched him slowly make his way across the road. The movements were familiar. But there was a difference.

No longer did I view him as just a person with disabilities who was unusual and wore movie-star-style reflective sunglasses and whose trademark was a mass of tattoos. I now saw him as a human being. Like myself. With personality. With feelings. With emotions.

Lost to my thoughts momentarily, I suddenly shuddered involuntarily. He hadn't just developed those characteristics. They'd been there all along—I simply hadn't bothered to take the time and effort to find out.

I felt condemned. Guilty.

MUSINGS AND OBSERVATIONS

Here's to a Good Year

I'm not just sure how it got started, but it seems that people around the world are addicted to making New Year's resolutions. Equally universal is the fact that a few minutes, hours, days, or weeks into the new year they find themselves ready to throw in the towel because they've failed to carry out their good intentions.

I've made resolutions of all kinds: to keep my desk clean and tidy, never to start a new task until I have completed the old one, to help my wife with the dishes more often, and the list goes on. I've even resolved not to make any more New Year's resolutions! But alas, the habit has become so ingrained that before I know what has happened, I've made a few more!

So is there anything we can do to make an upcoming year a more successful one? Can we actually follow through on what we really want to do? I think so.

Years ago I assisted with a number of stop-smoking plans, a community service that has helped several million people around the world kick the smoking habit. The interesting thing about the plans is that smokers are told to say, not "I will never smoke again," but "I *choose* not to smoke."

If they make the rash promise that they'll never smoke, they'll lose everything when they give in to the craving and have a puff. Then, having broken their promise, they're apt to give up altogether.

If they say they *choose* not to smoke, however, they've lost merely one battle in a long hard fight should they happen to take a drag or two on the weed. But they still *choose* not to smoke. And there's a big difference between losing a battle and losing the war.

The crucial element in any behavioral change is the power of choice, willpower. And to demonstrate this power, speakers at stop-smoking plans often compare willpower to the rudder of the old *Queen Elizabeth*. An 85,000-ton ship would obviously be fairly difficult to turn around. But despite the ship's mass, the rudder, though less than 1/1,000th of the total weight, can guide it. Our will, though seemingly insignificant, is the determining factor in what we do.

And how does all this relate to New Year's resolutions? Simply this: Suppose my resolution is to help my wife with the dishes regularly. But New Year's Day has been busy, and after supper I sit down in front of the TV and prop up my feet to watch my favorite program.

I'm just getting into the exciting part when I hear my wife clunking around in the kitchen doing the dishes. I'm faced with a choice. Do I really *choose* to help her with the dishes, as I have resolved? Or do I really choose to watch TV? If I truly choose to help, I'll get out of my chair and go to it—even if the TV program is only five minutes from its conclusion and she has only 10 spoons left to wash.

By doing that, I'll find it easier to remember and follow through on my resolution next time. If I choose instead to take the easier route, I'll be even less apt to remember next time, let alone do something about it.

The fact that I happened to have forgotten my resolution and to have sat down in front of the TV isn't the significant thing. What is significant is how I react when I become aware that I'm not doing what I had resolved to do. If I truly make up my mind to do it, if I truly direct my willpower that way, the actual doing is quite simple. The tough part is *choosing* to do it.

That is, I believe, the key to making and following through on resolutions—at New Year's or at any other time of the year.

MUSINGS AND OBSERVATIONS

If I Had It to Do Again

When I turned 35 I was brought face to face with my own mortality. Granted, a thirty-fifth birthday isn't traditionally thought of in the same sense as the eighteenth (the vote), twenty-first (adulthood), fortieth ("life begins at 40"), sixty-fifth (a well-deserved rest), or 100th (congratulations from the president or a royal telegram, depending on where you live).

Still, at 35 I was halfway through my "threescore and 10." And even today's wonder drugs haven't all that dramatically altered the statistics relating to the hourglass of life described several millennia ago.

It was sobering to think that my life was approximately half over if all went well—and perhaps considerably more than half over if tragedy struck. So I decided it was a good time to take stock. What would I do differently if I had the first half of my life to live again?

1. I'd keep a diary. Granted, when I was a teenager or even a young adult, I didn't feel like sitting down and writing out all my thoughts and observations. And once I started working, I thought I was too busy.

But I would love to be able to recall many of the questions I wrestled with as a youth and to be able to review the thought processes that lay behind my conclusions. What a help that would have been in my early years as a youth pastor. I think it would make me a more understanding parent as well.

I'd like to be able to relive my first impressions of the different cultures I've lived in: of Mexico as a 19-year-old volunteer schoolteacher; of England as a student; of Australia as a young pastor; of America as a returning expatriate. I would like to recall in detail the impact of the people I've met and the experiences I've had. It would be grist for a thousand stories or magazine articles or sermons. But most of it has slipped from memory.

2. I'd study foreign languages more diligently. Not only is learning a foreign language "the ultimate exercise in common courtesy," as a teacher once described it to me, but it also provides more insight into people and how they think and reason than perhaps any other study (besides, it's such a wonderful tool in travel and research and reading).

3. I'd read more. The Bible, religious writings, great literary works, history, the social sciences. I would seek more to derive my thoughts and actions and values from a broader base than my own limited experience.

4. I'd be more conscious of money. I would have guarded my finances—which have never been substantial. I would have saved and invested more.

I would have familiarized myself with the variety of ways available to make money work for you—not because I'm greedy or because money is greatly important to me or because I want to be rich. But because I have a moral obligation to do as much as possible with what I've been given. And because the realities of compounding interest mean that money invested early in life is of far more value to the investor than money invested later.

5. I'd be more sensitive to the feelings of others. Not that I was ever intentionally cruel or malicious. But I too often laughed with the crowd at the person who was slightly different.

I too often failed to stop and ask myself what I would do if I were in the other person's shoes. I too often assumed that if I could easily do something, then everyone else should be able to do so also. I too often was in too much of a hurry getting where I wanted to go in life to pay much attention to people who weren't headed the same direction or were simply moving more slowly and could have used a helping hand.

6. I'd spend more time in solitude, meditating, and reflecting. I would try to slow down, allowing more time for the Spirit to speak to me in the silence of my soul.

7. I'd never say that it was too late in life to start some project or to begin some habit that I felt was really necessary or worthwhile.

MUSINGS AND OBSERVATIONS

Less Than Meets the Eye

A few years ago I was browsing through my copy of *Bartlett's Familiar Quotations* when I happened upon a subtle insult reported in the writings of Alexander Woollcott.

It seems that Mr. Woollcott was watching a play when his companion, in a clever twist of a familiar expression, described his reaction to the play with the words, "There is less in this than meets the eye."

The phrase captured my fancy and has been running through my mind ever since—"There is *less* in this than meets the eye." And it has struck me that the phrase may be applicable to much of life today.

In general, we tend to spend our lives seeking pleasure, power, status, or money—or all four, as they often are closely linked. But usually there is less in these things than meets the eye.

Take status, for example. A few years ago I was at a gas station in Sydney, Australia, when a brand-new, immaculately polished Ford LTD pulled up to the gas pump next to me. The car was towing about as large a yacht—equally immaculate—as a car of that size could pull.

A well-dressed man got out, moving about with an air of self-importance as he ordered the attendant around and flashed his diamond ring as he paid. He obviously had "arrived" socially.

Well, not quite.

Just as he was about to get into his car and drive on down the road, what should pull into the station but the latest model Cadillac, imported from America, pulling an even larger yacht!

Maybe it was my imagination, but it seemed to me that the LTD owner suddenly lost some of his calm, cool, confident composure. And if I'm not mistaken, I saw a hint of jealousy in his look. There was less to his status than met the eye.

Power often is the same. People ignore their families, have no time for things once enjoyed, and develop ulcers as they climb to the top of the ladder—only to discover that it's toward the top that all the darts are hurled. Here, again, there usually is less satisfaction than meets the eye.

Furthermore—although we may try to kid ourselves—we could drop dead tomorrow, and the company would still keep running, the product would still come out more or less on schedule, the world would still go about its business. The nearest we come to being indispensable is to those who love us dearly. So why not concentrate more on them?

Similarly, many of our pleasures—which are usually self-centered—carry inherently negative side effects. Too many of our pleasures take us through a momentary high that leaves us down for the next few days. And we soon begin to say, "Is that all there is? Can't life give us anything better than this?"

Or we work and save for a trip to some exotic place, only to find it is not as good as the tourist brochure described it. Then we return home, tired and weary, saying, "Why did we waste the money?"

We save to buy some long-cherished item only to discover that it doesn't provide the sense of fulfillment we had expected—that there is less in it than meets the eye.

Pleasure, power, status, money—these things are not intrinsically bad. But, paradoxically, they bring far more satisfaction when they come as a by-product of a life dedicated to living for others rather than as a goal in their own right. Which suggests that in the case of living for others, there is actually more in it than meets the eye.

MUSINGS AND OBSERVATIONS

Metamorphosis

In nature we at times observe creatures going through a number of developmental stages before arriving at the level for which they were designed. Likewise, human beings often pass through stages before reaching the level of experience God desires for us. A prime example of this metamorphosis of character can be seen in the life of Moses.

Studying Moses' first 40 years, we encounter the Moses of manipulation. Having a sense of his own destiny, feeling that God has great things in store for him, acquiring the best education available, and enjoying a position from which he feels he can make great things happen, Moses sets about in his own might to accomplish the deliverance of the Hebrews.

But things do not go according to plan. And Moses ends this phase rushing into the desert like a frightened child running from danger.

Watching the second 40 years, we observe the Moses of meditation. Having failed in his own strength to accomplish his objectives and having been forced to flee to the desert of Midian because of a price on his head, Moses begins to understand that it's not might or power but God's Spirit that brings success. Thus, when invited to return to Egypt to undertake the mission to which he has felt called since his earliest recollections, he is overcome by the sense of his own inadequacy.

Finally, after having spent 40 years shielded from the artificialities of society and having developed an intimate acquaintance with his Creator, Moses becomes in the last 40 years of his life the Moses of mediation. Recognizing his human limitations, he's able to become a channel through whom God can pour out His blessings upon the Hebrews.

When the Hebrews are trapped at the Red Sea, God provides a way of escape through Moses. When water is scarce, Moses is the channel through whom a miracle is wrought. When a battle is being lost, victory comes through Moses' uplifted hands.

So Christlike is Moses in his love for the Hebrews that when the Lord suggests that they be destroyed, he requests that he be blotted out with them. It's not without reason that in Revelation 15 we read of a group of the redeemed singing the song of Moses and of the Lamb.

Each of us as Christians—and as Seventh-day Adventists in particular—has been called to fill a role not altogether different from that played by Moses. Each of us is to be a channel through whom God can bring deliverance to a world held captive by sin.

Thus, when that group of the redeemed sing the song of Moses and of the Lamb, it's not merely because they themselves have been delivered, but also because they've been allowed to be part of the deliverance process by being the carriers of the good news of salvation.

While we would hope that the manipulative stage of our experience would be short-lived (if not absent altogether), most of us, like Moses, must first grow to an understanding. We have to recognize the futility of attempting to accomplish great things in our strength before we'll come to God as meditative learners.

Then, having learned to trust in God's sufficiency, we, like Moses, can go forth to share His salvation with those around us.

MUSINGS AND OBSERVATIONS

Mirror, Mirror, on the Car

When my family and I moved to Australia in 1986, I had to go to the police station to register my car and arrange to take a test to get a driver's license.

One of our sons, Jared, who was 4 years old at the time, went with me. And whenever Jared was with me, silence was not.

I must say, just to put you into the picture, that in the town to which we had moved, 90 per cent of all buildings were built on hillsides. And 90 percent of the time it was raining. So, true to form, the police station was perched on a rather steep hill. And it was literally pouring when I arrived.

Because the police-station drive was slightly difficult to negotiate, I chose to back up the drive (with emphasis on *up*). Jared was asking his usual questions: "Why would they build a station on such a hill? Do police in Warburton ride in cars or on motorbikes? Why don't they use boats?" And so on.

Everything was going nicely. Then, suddenly, a harmless-looking railing (after having conned me into thinking it was two feet farther over than it was), without provocation and without warning, leaped out and brutally ripped off one of my side mirrors!

At best, crashing into something is humiliating. But did it have to happen when Jared was with me? I mean, he was one of the very few people in the world who still believed that I was anywhere near perfect. But it wasn't the rude awakening he would experience concerning my fallibility that chagrined me most: it was what he would tell his mother.

Before I was even out of the car when we arrived home, he was halfway up the stairs. "Mommy! Mommy! Daddy wrecked the car in front of the police station!" So much for being able to lord it over her about my driving superiority.

Of course, that all came later. What I dreaded at that moment was having to walk into the police station. Perhaps they hadn't heard, I told myself. But no such luck. The door to the station had been wide open. Since they had heard, I went ahead and confessed, simply to put the whole thing in the best light possible.

As I have reflected on this humiliating ordeal—which, without question, is the worst thing that had happened to me since I fell down a set of stairs while a half dozen dignitaries from the General Conference looked on—I have come to the conclusion that ripping the mirror off my car was really no big thing. The real problem was having people *know* what I had done.

And as I've reflected, it has struck me that in much the same way far too many of us would readily do little things—or even big things—we know to be wrong if we could guarantee that no one would ever find out about it. Our real restraint is often not our sterling characters but our concern for our public image.

In contrast, I think of the story of Joseph. When tempted, he didn't say, "Oh, but what if we get caught?" No, he said, "How then can I do this great wickedness, and sin against God?" Right and wrong, not public image, should be *our* concern too.

While that's true with respect to morality, I hope you will be just a little bit tolerant when I tell you that when I actually went to take the driving test, I was praying that the officer who administered it wouldn't be the same one who was on duty when I visited the station the first time!

MUSINGS AND OBSERVATIONS

Motives

He came home late, exhausted. Eyelids heavy, he scarcely could remove his contact lenses. Then he couldn't find their container. Oh well, a cup would do. He set it high on the window ledge. No chance that anyone would disturb it before he got up.

She got up early—very early. Seeing the dirty dishes, she decided to do them to surprise her parents. She did them all, even though she was only 8. Any more? Ah, one more, high on the window ledge.

"Sarah, did you see a red cup near the window?"

"Yes, Daddy. I thought I'd surprise you, so I washed all the dishes. I almost missed that one, though."

He never told her. He just bit his tongue—and bought new contacts.

We all know people who do the *right* thing for the *wrong* reason. What we often fail to realize is that multitudes of people do the *wrong* thing for the *right* reason. Sincere but misguided behavior doesn't reside exclusively in the domain of children. Although childish mistakes may elicit tolerant smiles, adults are equally prone to poor judgment—and they often are judged quite harshly as a result.

Peter no doubt was sincere in his rash act of cutting off the ear of the high priest's servant in Gethsemane. The act—though misguided—probably reflected a genuine concern for Jesus' safety.

The pastor who tells an unwed mother-to-be that her pregnancy is God's way of punishing her for her fornication may believe what he's saying and feel that he must help her understand the seriousness of her transgression.

The dear saint who suggests that a shabbily dressed person should don better apparel or not desecrate the church with his presence may have strong convictions about worship and reverence for God.

No doubt many members of the Inquisition believed that they were doing God a great favor by ridding the land of heretics. And similar atrocities carried out by Protestants against Catholics and against each other could claim equally laudable motivation.

While we may recognize the devastation caused by such mistakes in judgment, and while we may even be able to show the moral repugnance of certain actions, it isn't our responsibility to determine the motive behind the behavior. "Man looketh on the outward appearance, but the Lord looketh on the heart" (1 Samuel 16:7).

We may pride ourselves on our individual wisdom and on the amassed wisdom of the age in which we live, but we, in fact, all view reality in a manner not altogether different from the perspectives of a child. We all see "through a glass, darkly" (1 Corinthians 13:12). And were the results of our actions not so tragic, even our most enlightened behavior no doubt at times would seem comical to the onlooking intelligent beings of the universe.

Recognition of our finiteness should compel us to seek God's wisdom so that we might see as He sees. As our blurred vision clears, our treatment of others will become more what Christ would have it to be. Such treatment will include a great degree of tolerance for many people, who on the surface may appear reprehensible, but who in reality are merely sincere bunglers.

MUSINGS AND OBSERVATIONS

Not Staying

Several years ago a minister friend of mine was visiting the publishing house where I worked. As he had no transportation to where he was headed for lunch, I offered him a lift.

"Well," he said as soon as he got into my car, "it looks like you're not planning to stick around here long—driving an old bomb like this. Whenever I drove an old car, it meant I planned to move on soon. You really should get yourself something a little more representative, you know."

"As a matter of fact," I said—as soon as I'd swallowed three times, double-checked that my ears were functioning, and caught my breath enough to speak—"this happens to be the most expensive car I've ever owned." Then, as quickly as possible, I changed the subject.

But the man's comments lingered in my mind. True, my car didn't hold a candle to what some ministers drive. But I certainly didn't see it as an "old bomb." I mean, it still was less than a decade old. It was reliable. It had no dents and no rust. The upholstery had no major stains or tears. It had no rattles. And the tires had plenty of tread. The only major flaw in its appearance that I was aware of was that the dashboard had a bit of "skin cancer" from too much time basking in the sunshine.

But what am I trying to prove by citing all these details about my car? Simply this: Western society in general and the media in particular put tremendous pressures on us to keep up with the Joneses, to climb the social ladder, to indulge in conspicuous consumption. And unfortunately, similar subtle and not-so-subtle pressure can also come right from within our own church—which should be a haven from such artificiality.

While pastoring in the suburb of a large city, I made it a point to visit the 15 or 20 other congregations and synagogues in the vicinity. I discovered that the people in my congregation were more expensively ("representatively"?) dressed than were the members of any of the other congregations in the affluent area where my church was situated.

True, the women in those other churches wore their makeup more visibly. And they definitely wore more jewelry. But neither the women nor the men projected as consistent a middle- to upper-class image as did my parishioners—not even in their cars.

Now, we could argue that Adventists' material prosperity is the reward for loyalty to God and good stewardship—which is partially true. Further, our visible prosperity may attract others to our faith.

But every coin has a flip side. And many poorer people feel that they wouldn't be welcome in some Adventist congregations. In fact, I've heard several young Adventist couples say they feel they just can't keep up with what seems to be the expectation in the churches they attend.

The question is How much do we *really* need? Adequate food—but it needn't be fancy or costly. Functional, durable, tasteful clothing—but it needn't be the latest European fashion. A place we can call home—but it needn't be the size of a football field. Reliable transportation that gets us from A to B in reasonable comfort—but it needn't turn the heads of others. And the list goes on.

Unfortunately, in today's society things that should be merely functional have become associated with status and success. Thus we find ourselves on a merry-go-round of unnecessary financial pressure.

I'm convinced, for example, that a high percentage of us could live as easily on one wage as our parents did a few decades ago. The difference is purely a matter of how much we feel we must have. We're not prepared to live as they did. Yesterday's dreams have become today's necessities.

I'm not trying to dictate how anyone should eat, where they should live, what they should wear, or how they should transport themselves from A to B. However, as I've reflected on my friend's comment, I've become convinced that the best way we could say that we believe Jesus is coming soon is by giving the clear impression that we really don't plan to stick around here long.

FACTS AND FABLES

Against Sin or *for* Righteousness?

To the casual observer it might seem that being *against* sin is synonymous with being *for* righteousness. And certainly the Christian should be both.

Nonetheless, an imbalance in emphasis can mean the difference between a negative and a positive identity, a religion that stifles and one that fulfills, a message that repels and one that attracts.

Unfortunately, too many of us have tended to enunciate our faith in terms of the negative: we don't smoke, we don't drink, we don't dance, we don't work on Saturday. While it may be true that we *don't* do these things, the significant thing is what we *do*.

Our religion should be more a matter of experiencing the good than of not experiencing the bad. It should be more a matter of seeking optimum health than of merely abstaining from unwholesome foods. It should be more a matter of uninterrupted communion with God on the Sabbath than of not working. It should be more a matter of seeking to receive the seal of God than of avoiding the mark of the beast.

Because of our all-too-frequent tendency to present attractive opportunities as if they were galling obligations, because of a failure to present our beliefs in a positive context, Seventh-day Adventists have been accused of being legalistic. And periodically throughout our history, individuals have felt constrained to break away from the church to pursue a course free from such an emphasis.

Ironically, these individuals, while ostensibly deriving their identity from a pure and positive Christ-centered gospel, frequently have succumbed to the pitfall they once detested—that of placing more emphasis upon what is opposed than upon what is advocated. Often their primary identifying mark is that they're *not* Seventh-day Adventists. Inadvertently, they too are more *against* than *for.*

While we shouldn't cease to shun sin, it's imperative that we pursue righteousness. Only then can we truly experience that abundant life that Christ came to give. Only in the preaching and practice of righteousness do we find a totally positive identity, a fulfilling and liberating religion, and a message that will attract with a supernatural power.

FACTS AND FABLES

Bringing Up Junior

When I was a young pastor, just married and fresh out of college, I had an exceptional understanding of what constituted good child rearing. And I was quite willing to share my knowledge—if asked, of course.

By the time I was ordained, my wife and I had one child. And through some inexplicable process, my wisdom had diminished considerably. As a result, I was more reticent to share it with others.

Now we have three boys and have experienced every challenge from toddler to teenager to young adult. And it just struck me the other day that if I'm ever going to write about child rearing, I'd better get on with it, or I'm going to have nothing to say at all—let alone be willing to say it!

Of the vast store of knowledge to which I once laid claim, only three points remain: 1. All children are different. 2. Heredity plays a greater role than many of us would like to admit. 3. Even perfect parents (if such a species exists!) do not necessarily have perfect offspring.

1. The first point may seem trite. Of course all children are different. Of course they have unique personalities, varied talents, their own likes and dislikes. Yet no sooner do the words leave our mouths than we turn around and try to use a one-size-fits-all formula in dealing with them.

The simple fact is that while there are basic principles of human behavior, there's no magic formula that works in all cases—or even in most cases.

One child may respond to a firm approach; the child's twin may be reduced to sobs by the same treatment. One child may need to be liberated from his or her inhibitions; another may need to be calmed down. One child may need to learn that he or she *does* have talents; another may need to learn that *others* have talents too.

Simply put, children can never be assembly-line products; they all must be custom-built—on a foundation already provided.

2. Those parents whose children are always well behaved and who have never had the problems many of their neighbors have faced may not like my second point. But those who have raised one or two children who were angels, and another one or two who were major challenges from square one, will find themselves in agreement: To a great degree children are what they are from birth. From conception, I should say.

One of our boys was on the move constantly from the time he was about 4½ months old—at which time he learned to do a modified military low crawl. In fact, he refused to stop moving even to have his diaper changed. And eventually, rather than go through the terrible ordeal of trying to keep him pinned down on his back, we learned to change his diaper while he was on the move—much to the consternation of one onlooker, who had raised a near-perfect child through having followed the right formula.

But when the onlooker's second child came along, the formula went awry. In one letter she admitted that it had been one of the most humbling experiences of her life. Here she thought her earlier success had been skill, but it now appeared that it might not have been. And to top it off, she had even stooped to the level of sometimes changing her child's diaper while he was on the move rather than face the ordeal of trying to fight him onto his back!

3. Finally, parents often take too much responsibility for their children's behavior. When children grow up to be law-abiding, God-fearing, decent adults, parents should praise God and humbly acknowledge that it might have been more *in spite* of than *because* of the role they played.

Conversely, should our children not turn out to be pillars of society, should their lives not be what we would have hoped for them, I believe we should be careful in blaming ourselves too severely. Remember, the world's first "children," in a perfect environment, went bad.

Does that mean that God failed?

FACTS AND FABLES

Devil's Doctrine

Several years ago I heard a minister tell of a young girl he met during a Week of Prayer. At the closing meeting many of the young folk were giving public testimonies of what Christ had done for them. And some were giving their hearts to God for the first time.

Finally, toward the end of the meeting and after considerable urging from others, the young girl in question stood to her feet. With tears running down her cheeks she said, "I know that Jesus is coming soon, and I'd better give my heart to God. But I don't expect ever to have another day of fun in life."

Childishness, you say? Perhaps. Yet all too often Christians—particularly Seventh-day Adventists—spend too much time talking about how much they have to sacrifice to be Christians.

I've heard many people talk about the high-paying or prestigious careers they've given up to follow Christ. So what? I've heard ministers describe how much they could make if they weren't ministers. So what?

If these people do not find following Christ or ministering for Him infinitely more rewarding than money and prestige, then by all means they should get on with what really would make them happy. On the other hand, if having that money and prestige wouldn't make them happier, if it actually is inferior to what they have, doesn't it seem strange that they even bring up the subject?

How many people walk away from a delectable meal saying, "Well, that was a good meal, but eating it meant that I had to give up my hunger"? How many people complain about having to give up their thirst when they've received a cool, refreshing drink on a hot day? Or is it only when we question the real worth of what we have that we begin to look back and say, "Well, I did have to give up . . ."?

The Christian should be able to say the words of the apostle Paul (originally spoken in a different context, but true here nonetheless): "For his sake I have suffered the loss of all things, and count them as refuse, in order that I may gain Christ" (Philippians 3:8, RSV).

Has the Christian ever been asked to give up anything that, in comparison with what God gives in its place, wouldn't seem about as valuable as refuse?

Jesus said, "There is no one who has left house or brothers or sisters or mother or father or children or lands, for my sake and for the gospel, who will not receive a hundredfold now in this time, houses and brothers and sisters and mothers and children and lands, with persecutions, and in the age to come eternal life" (Mark 10:29, 30, RSV).

While Christ doesn't promise a bed of roses to His followers, He makes it clear that despite the persecution and hardship we may have to suffer for our faith, life right here and now is still at least 100 times better than if we hadn't come to know Him. As if that weren't enough, eternal life is thrown in as a bonus.

We should be very hesitant about suggesting that Christians are called upon to make sacrifices. True, we may not have a fancy car or a fancy house because we choose to give that money for missions. But isn't the thrill of spreading the gospel greater fulfillment than can be found in fancy cars or houses?

We may feel called by God to serve in a remote area as a missionary. But isn't the joy of such service, of knowing that we're playing a vital role in presenting Christ to the world, an honor that far surpasses the rewards enjoyed by the bulk of the population? Doesn't it more than compensate for the separation from family, the relatively meager salary, and the absence of many of the modern conveniences?

In fact, granted that the early Christians believed that Jesus was the longed-for Messiah and that He had asked them to serve and honor Him come what may—wasn't it a lesser sacrifice for them to face the lions than to have to live the rest of their lives hating themselves for not having had the courage to stand up for what they believed to be truth? Which really is the greater sacrifice?

I'm not suggesting that the pain and suffering of these martyrs wasn't horrible beyond imagination. But while their bodies were ravaged, their consciences remained clear. They were following in the steps of their beloved Master, and they actually spoke as if it were a privilege (1 Peter 4:12-16; Acts 5:41; Philippians 1:29).

Perhaps we could take this theme one step further. Granted that God's very nature is love, a love so deep that it does not cease even when humans fall into the most vile sin, wouldn't it have been a lesser sacrifice for Christ to come to die for us than it would have been for Him to have left us to our own devices, to have abandoned us eternally?

Again, this in no way diminishes the magnitude of what Christ has done. To the contrary. It shows the infinite depth of His love—that He would prefer a life of persecution and an ignominious death to living in peace and glory without us.

Despite the horrors He suffered, Christ never burdened His followers with long rehearsals of what He had to give up to come to this earth to rescue humanity from sin. Christ came because He loved us, because the joy that was set before Him—the joy of seeing lost humanity once again restored to its proper place—was reward enough. If Christ didn't dwell upon His sacrifice, then certainly we shouldn't.

The options we face aren't always pleasant. We live not in utopia but in a world of sin. Often none of the possibilities before us are ideal. But I'd suggest that, granted the realities with which we have to deal, the Christian is seldom, if ever, called upon to make a sacrifice. Instead, he or she is always asked to choose the best, most fulfilling option available.

It's time that we as Adventists cease talking about how much we've had to sacrifice, and concentrate instead on how much we've received. Let's take the word *sacrifice* out of our glossary of acceptable terminology and call it what it is—simply another devil's doctrine.

FACTS AND FABLES

Facing the Fact of Life

For many years I fell victim to a detached objectivity as I watched pro-life forces battle it out with those advocating pro-choice in the abortion debate. You see, the issue really was of no direct concern to me.

First, I'm male. Further, as a person of sterling character who has a chaste approach to things sexual (and who can blind people with my self-styled halo), I would surely have no worries about out-of-wedlock pregnancy. And as for unwanted pregnancy within marriage, there's little excuse for that these days. In short, I probably viewed abortion as a problem of the promiscuous and the careless.

Now, don't get me wrong. Liking a good argument, I found abortion a great topic for academic discussions—as long as nobody went into too graphic detail about the process. Particularly when we were eating.

But increasingly I'm the finding the topic more upsetting, even when I'm not eating. And it has a lot to do with what I believe about the fact of life.

The abortion issue is complex. Whether we like it or not, 10- and 12-year-old girls do become pregnant. Women and girls are raped. Incest does occur. Abnormalities do develop. The continued growth of a fetus does, at times, threaten a mother's life.

On the other hand, should we allow the complexity of a relatively few cases to overcomplicate the vast majority of cases? Do we let the exception dictate our approach to the norm?

Most abortions have nothing to do with 10- and 12-year-old girls, or rape, or incest, or abnormalities, or direct threat to the life of the mother. They have to do with unwanted pregnancy. With convenience and inconvenience.

Modern technology has removed most of the physical danger of abortion, and our current approach to ethics has whitewashed its moral danger. You see, we still—conveniently—haven't determined precisely when life begins.

As long as we can remain uncertain on this point, we can keep our consciences clear by telling ourselves that abortion doesn't really take *life*. After all, it's really nothing more than a blob of tissue growing in a woman's uterus.

We also studiously avoid referring to that blob as a human being, or even a potential human being. Such references introduce the element of emotion, making "objective" decisions about "its" continued existence more difficult.

The fact that not many weeks after the fetus started growing it began to develop arms, legs, and genitals is incidental. The fact that a little heart is beating in a little chest is irrelevant. The fact that those rapidly dividing cells contain the total genetic program of a unique human being is also of no consequence. "Viability" is the watchword. If it isn't viable, it mustn't be a living human being.

But what do we mean by viability? Viability has to be a relative term. For example, is a baby at full term but who doesn't receive attention and care from others any more viable than a fetus? Is any unclad human viable in arctic conditions?

Is an elderly person viable if unable to attend to his or her own needs? Is the doctor performing an abortion viable if he or she is deprived of oxygen for a half hour? Or does viability presuppose an appropriate environment and support system?

Why can't we stop the mental and moral gymnastics? Why must we resort to "abortionspeak" to avoid certain unpleasant feelings that otherwise are inevitable?

Why can't we simply admit that this "intrauterine tissue growth"—or whatever other euphemism we wish to use—is in fact a living human being? Having acknowledged that, we can then look at whether the circumstances justify killing this *person*. And they may. Or they may not.

Most societies have decided that killing in war is—at times, at least—justifiable (though I question that conclusion). And many societies have also determined that criminals guilty of certain offenses should be deprived of life (though I question that conclusion as well).

But at least when we kill in these circumstances we're courageous enough to acknowledge what we're doing. We don't suggest that criminals, or those who happen to be on the opposing side in war, may not be truly alive or truly human. We simply acknowledge such killing as a dirty job that has to be done. And we get on with it.

Similarly, there may be times when taking unborn life is the lesser evil of the unsatisfactory options available to us. But I believe the times are few. And I believe it is taking *life*.

If we adequately explained the *facts* of life—both biological and moral—the number of people who ever have to make a decision about abortion would diminish greatly. And if we squarely faced the *fact* of life—that it is *life*—most abortion clinics would go out of business.

FACTS AND FABLES

Facts and Faith

"A *little learning is a dangerous thing;/ Drink deep, or taste not the Pierian spring:/ There shallow draughts intoxicate the brain,/ And drinking largely sobers us again."—Alexander Pope.*

A few years ago I was privileged to participate in a geoscience field conference conducted in the South Pacific Division by the General Conference's Geoscience Research Institute.

As I sat through hours of lectures, and as we observed firsthand various phenomena that are often used to support either the creation-flood model or an evolutionary model of origins, four things stood out in my nonscientific mind.

First, I was impressed, as never before, by the power of nature. For example, current scientific thinking suggests that such mountain ranges as the Southern Alps of New Zealand and the Andes are the result of upthrust caused by huge pieces of the earth's crust bumping against each other.

These mountains constitute tens of thousands of cubic kilometers of rock. Yet the forces of nature have moved them around almost as if they were pebbles.

During the conference we learned how when large volcanoes erupt, they often eject many cubic kilometers of material, spewing it several kilometers into the air. The topography of huge regions can be changed overnight. And throughout the history of this earth, such eruptions have happened time and time again.

And these are but a few examples of nature's awesome power.

Second, as I sat through the lectures and listened to lecturers discuss the merits of the various explanations scientists put forward to explain certain observable geophysical phenomena, it struck me how little really we know with certainty—all our scientific knowledge notwithstanding.

For even when we can provide impressive data to back our assumptions concerning origins, and even when we can set up laboratory experiments to demonstrate that certain mechanisms provide plausible explanations, in the final analysis we cannot prove that the scenario we describe is in fact what actually transpired. It might have come about by any number of other means.

Whether we use the creation-flood model or the evolutionary model to explain origins, in the end we must make a leap of faith. The geoscience field conference convinced me more than ever that I need not be ashamed for having chosen to believe in fiat creation by God. I learned of more data to support that position than I had been aware of before.

On the other hand, the experience also waved a warning flag against overconfidence. While the creation-flood model provides adequate scientific explanations for many of the phenomena science has observed, there are also many phenomena that it currently cannot explain.

Thus, we must guard against making it appear that we have more hard data than we in fact have. We must never forget the faith component in what we believe about origins.

Third, the more I see of the complexity of the universe, particularly the complexity of living organisms, the more convinced I become that there had to be a Designer. Truly, we are "fearfully and wonderfully made" (Psalm 139:14).

Fourth, and finally, when I look out at the starry heavens, and when I hear scientists describing the magnitude of the universe, I stand in awe, asking with the psalmist, "What is man, that thou art mindful of him? and the son of man, that thou visitest him?" (Psalm 8:4).

FACTS AND FABLES

Fat and Other Weighty Issues

Nursery-rhyme character Jack Sprat isn't alone in his aversion to fat. It seems that governments have jumped onto the bandwagon, too.

Some years ago the state parliament of New South Wales, Australia, heard a report that 200-pounds-plus Sue and Michael Murname had been told that they were too fat to adopt a baby—despite the fact that according to a spokesperson for the New South Wales Youth and Community Services minister, the couple was "fine" in every category evaluated (except girth).

"I know they're saying that being overweight might affect our health in the future," said Mrs. Murname, "but we've been told by our doctor that we're both fit. [And] how can anyone guarantee they'll be healthy for the next 15 or 20 years?"

Undoubtedly, the state has an interest in making certain that potential adoptive parents are not high risks for ill health or early death. And obesity has been determined to be a contributor to both.

The state's decision, however, highlights the fact that it is the definable and documentable inadequacy that usually gets the attention, irrespective of whether or not it's the most significant shortfall.

Fat, for example, is an objective reality that's difficult to disguise. Yet temper, sarcasm, and a host of other forms of behavior that might be more detrimental to a child's development and long-term welfare could easily go unnoticed.

In judging spiritual fitness, we as Adventists tend to employ an evaluation system that likewise focuses almost exclusively on that which is readily apparent and easily documentable—although, because we're more concerned with actions than with states of being, fat wouldn't rate major consideration in our system.

For example, as Adventists we advocate total abstinence from alcoholic beverages, making it a "test of fellowship." However, the Bible makes equally strong comments about both gluttons and drunkards. Yet to my knowledge no one has ever been refused admission to or been disfellowshipped from the Adventist Church for being a glutton—and there must be a few in our midst.

The difference between drinking and gluttony is that drinking is an overt, easily definable act. Gluttony, on the other hand, is extremely difficult to identify. Because of body metabolism and numerous other factors, fat may not indicate gluttony's presence, and thinness in no way suggests its absence.

With drinking alcohol, we can condemn the act entirely. With gluttony, it's a matter of degree—too much of a *good* thing.

Our inability to define and identify either in ourselves or others a wide range of sins—some that involve actions, some that involve thoughts and attitudes—means that we: (1) fail to denounce them adequately or provide adequate assistance in helping people overcome them; and, as a result, (2) think of ourselves as being quite upright as long as we're succumbing only to elusive sins and not to those that by their very nature are more observable and clearly definable as sin.

We should note, however, that in Matthew 23 Jesus denounced the scribes and Pharisees for concentrating on the observable—such as tithing—to the exclusion of many things that actually were more crucial to spiritual health but that were more difficult to identify, such as judgment and mercy and faith.

I'm not suggesting that we relax any of our church standards. Nor am I suggesting that we should go on witch hunts to seek out those who are slaves to hidden sins. What I am saying is that an absence of any glaring spiritual inadequacies may not tell us very much about our true spiritual condition.

FACTS AND FABLES

If You Were Truly Sincere

Recently a young woman, not a Seventh-day Adventist, attended an Adventist church with friends. On the day of her visit the Sabbath school discussion centered around proper Sabbath observance. Some of the class members maintained that circumstances might justify a purchase on Sabbath. Others supported a more rigid view.

The visitor, who came from an evangelical background, graciously suggested that perhaps the class wasn't addressing the most significant point. She mentioned the theological hairsplitting over the same type of issues that occurred during the time of Christ. And she explained that to her the Sabbath was an experience, an interaction with God, and that this relationship took precedence over the beginning time, ending time, and activities throughout.

Having so spoken, she suddenly discovered that the formerly polarized class had achieved absolute unanimity. While they might debate the minutiae of how the Sabbath should be observed, they weren't prepared to tolerate heresy within their midst.

Making passing reference to a number of texts that support the Sabbath, and arguing for the perpetuity of God's law, the members firmly told the visitor that if she were truly sincere, she would see and accept the Sabbath truth—which conversely implied that if she failed to accept it she wasn't sincere.

The if-you-were-truly-sincere argument so often bandied about needs to be examined carefully. While it undoubtedly contains an element of truth, it has been greatly misused.

1. The discovery of truth is an ongoing process. Jesus said, "When he, the Spirit of truth, is come, he will guide you into all truth" (John 16:13).

The disciples had been with Christ more than three years, but they didn't have all truth. In fact, new truths will be unfolding throughout eternity.

2. Can we say that the apostles weren't sincere because they for so long failed to understand the true nature of Christ's mission? Was Peter insincere because he failed to understand the completeness of God's acceptance of the Gentiles—even after God had given him a vision concerning the subject?

Was William Miller not sincere when he ignored Jesus' statement that no man knows the day or hour of Christ's coming, and went ahead and set a date anyway? Was Ellen White not sincere because she didn't immediately accept the biblical prohibition of unclean meats? Or because initially she didn't recognize that the Sabbath should be kept from sunset to sunset?

3. While we as Adventists have taught that the Sabbath will play a major role in the closing events of earth's history and that the Sabbath ultimately will become a decisive test of loyalty, *The Great Controversy* makes it clear that we'll move into that era only shortly before Christ's return. At that time issues will become so clear that a rejection of the Sabbath will be synonymous with rejecting God. But we haven't entered that era yet.

4. We need to appreciate the difficulty humans encounter in changing deeply entrenched attitudes. Although it's a paradox, the more one has studied and developed a system of thought, the more difficult it is to accept a radically new position. The most solid adherents to any ideology are the least likely to convert to another ideology. But can we call it a lack of sincerity?

5. Although Christians have been told to make judgments in certain areas, and while we as Adventists believe that we'll be involved in judgment more fully during the millennium, it's Christ's exclusive prerogative to judge motive and sincerity. Furthermore, we're specifically warned against judging others.

6. The if-you-were-truly-sincere bullet can be fired from more than one gun. The very bullet that we have fired with such confidence may be fired back, bearing the inscription that we ourselves put on it—but now altered to read: "If you were truly sincere, you would demonstrate a more charitable attitude toward those who hold an opinion differing from your own. After all, didn't Christ have quite a bit to say about that, too?"

FACTS AND FABLES

Myth of the Open Mind

Over the years I've heard many Adventists say something such as "If searchers for spiritual truth would read the Bible with an open mind, without preconceptions and without prejudice, they would arrive at the same conclusions that we as Adventists have."

For years that statement gave me great confidence. But of more recent time it has caused me concern. For starters, it means that some 1.2 billion non-Adventist Christians don't have open minds, haven't studied their Bibles, or are dishonest.

If the statement is true, it leads to other questions. Why did Martin Luther reject the truths presented by some of the more radical reformers of his day—truths that we as Adventists now feel are important? And why did William Miller never accept the Sabbath? Were Luther and Miller not open-minded? Were they prejudiced? Did they just need more time?

Open-mindedness is a goal toward which we all should strive. But let's not delude ourselves that it can be easily achieved. Or that we have achieved it. Each of us is riddled with preconceptions.

Let's take the case of language. Not only does it *reflect* the way we see things; it also to a great degree *determines* how we see them.

To take an extreme example, the English language has a clear sense of movement through linear time. We have past, present, and future verb tenses. That makes it easy for us to relate to biblical prophecies that speak about periods of time.

But some languages don't have the sense of linear time that we find in English (or Hebrew and Greek). Time may be cyclical or circular. Or, as is the case with at least one American Indian language, there may be virtually no sense of time at all. Trying to explain some of the Bible's time prophecies to these people, in their own language, poses a major challenge.

Culture also plays a major role in molding our thoughts and perceptions—indeed, even our ability to perceive. And for the most part, it does so without our realizing that it's happening.

Also, personal experience influences us strongly. Take, for example, an Egyptian woman we'll call Jenny Smith (because I can't spell Egyptian names). In her entire lifetime she has met only 10 people calling themselves Christians—and all of them were greedy, self-serving, profane, immoral, and bigoted. She could scarcely be called closed-minded simply because she doesn't want to hear any more about Christianity.

And even education, which is supposed to broaden our minds, by its very nature also closes them. For instance, in most Western educational systems students are taught to establish a hypothesis, then gather data to prove or disprove it.

Inevitably this approach will carry over into their search for spiritual truth. Thus, even if it were possible for students versed in this educational method to approach Scripture without bias or preconception—which it isn't—they would immediately begin to look for patterns.

When they detected what they thought were patterns, they would form hypotheses. And from that point onward—be it at Genesis or John—everything would be read with a view to proving or disproving the hypothesis. And a hypothesis is nothing more than an educated preconception.

Too many of us have been too glib in our statements about the self-evident nature of truth. On the other hand, as we see the complexity of forces that mold our thoughts and perceptions, it would be equally easy to fall into the trap of determinism.

All of us are greatly influenced by language, culture, experience, education, and numerous other factors. But God's Spirit is more powerful still. He can break through the most formidable barriers.

But when, because of His guiding, we escape some of the bonds that limit our vision, let's not pat ourselves on the back as if it were because of our own innate goodness (or open-mindedness). Rather, let's humbly thank God for bringing us to "this place of highest privilege where we now stand" (Romans 5:2, TLB).

FACTS AND FABLES

Screening the Big Screen

I know that many people, for quite varied reasons, won't like what I have to say. But there are times when a person feels compelled to "tell it like it is."

My subject is attendance at the movie theater. And, to put it bluntly, we have lost the war in convincing Adventist young people that it's wrong.

I have no empirical evidence concerning the number of Adventists 50 years of age and younger who watch at least the occasional movie at the theater. But my dealings with this age group and the number of comments I pick up in casual conversation suggest to me that they number somewhere between 60 and 90 percent.

While most of these people don't flaunt their theater attendance, neither do they hide it. And the problem isn't limited to those younger than 50. So, as I see it, we have four possible responses.

First, we can bury our heads and pretend that the problem doesn't exist, or that it doesn't exist to the degree that I am suggesting. We can continue to refrain from addressing the real situation.

But the greater the gulf between Adventist behavior and the paper statements of what our behavior is supposed to be, the greater the church's loss of credibility.

Second, we can try to rally the forces and bolster our current stance—that discretion is the watchword in what we view at home and in the church hall, but that total abstinence is required when it comes to the theater.

There are at least two problems, however. 1. The majority of those 50 and younger simply don't buy the arguments (that older generations seem to have found convincing) about a difference between the lounge room, the church hall, and the theater. 2. A significant number of Adventist ministers themselves attend selected movies at the theater. And an even larger number find the above-mentioned distinction difficult to defend.

Third, we can acknowledge that there's no real distinction between the lounge room, the church hall, and the theater. We can take the position that, in fact, it's the *medium* that's bad—and that TV, films at the church hall, and films at the theater should *all* be declared unacceptable.

But this stance would require significant behavior modification on the part of many older Adventists. And they're no more willing than younger Adventists to sacrifice what to them is totally acceptable and defensible—if properly controlled.

Furthermore, were the church to take such a stand, it would imply that our traditional position has been wrong. And might not the realization that we've been wrong in one area lead members to question many other positions?

Also, might it not seem narrow-minded and arbitrary to ban all forms of the visual media categorically? Are we prepared to sacrifice *It Is Written?*

Fourth, we can take a pragmatic approach. Because most Adventists view films at the church hall and have televisions in their homes, and because a high percentage now attend the theater, we can accept what appears to be the inevitable and go all out to guide the trend rather than trying to stop it.

We can emphasize the need for discretion in viewing—wherever the viewing takes place. We can try to equip members to know how to assess what's good and what's bad.

But the implications of such a stance are far-reaching. As with point 3, it would mean admitting that we were wrong before. It would place unprecedented responsibility on the individual for moral decision-making. And these are but starters.

I'm not here prescribing which option is preferable. But if we continue trying to ignore the issue, we'll continue to go nowhere—except backward. Quickly.

FACTS AND FABLES

Seeking a More Secure Knot

When I stumble across friends from high school and college and we update each other about classmates, the inevitable question arises: Are they still married? The answer frequently is no.

Unfortunately, the Adventist Church closely reflects the high incidence of marital breakdown in the general populace. Of course, we can shrug it off and say it's merely a sign of the times. After all, didn't Jesus say that the end-time would be characterized by much marrying (Matthew 24:37, 38)? And doesn't that imply much divorce?

Divorce certainly isn't unique to our era. It was present at the time of Moses—and he sought to rein it in. It was present at the time of Jesus—and He sought to rein it in. And it's even more rampant today—but what are Adventists doing to rein it in?

Because the human heart is by nature legalistic, we look for loopholes that allow us to satisfy the letter of the law while still indulging in what the law prohibits. In Christ's day the loophole involved an elastic interpretation of what constituted "some uncleanness" in a woman—which was the prerequisite for an "acceptable" divorce (Deuteronomy 24:1).

Jesus plugged that loophole so effectively (Matthew 19:8-10) that His disciples threw up their hands in horror and said, "If you're going to make it *that* difficult to get a divorce, we'd be better off not to even marry!" And Jesus wasn't even trying to give a comprehensive theological statement on marriage. He was simply attacking one aberration.

Because human nature hasn't changed in the intervening 2,000 years, members of the Adventist Church today still look for loopholes. So in dealing with marriages that break up for reasons other than adultery, we've sheltered behind one small part of Christ's statement—*"and shall marry another."* Those four words have become the main focus.

The marriage vow assented to by most Adventist husbands and wives specifies a number of mutual responsibilities—"to have, to hold, to love, to honor, to cherish, so long as we both shall live." The parties also agree to abstain from all others.

Isn't it ironic that an Adventist can default on the "to have, to hold, to love, to honor, to cherish" part of the contract, yet run no risk of church discipline?

More ironic, the person can default on the "so long as we both shall live" part of the contract (by getting a divorce), and still not face church discipline. But the moment the person defaults on the last part (by remarrying) of this solemn contract sworn before God, church discipline becomes quite likely (at least in "hard-line" congregations).

By taking this stance, the church's unintended statement is: We're not terribly concerned about marriage, and we're not even that concerned about divorce. But we're adamantly opposed to remarriage after divorce.

We won't make a big issue of your leaving your spouse unfulfilled and miserable. In fact, we'll even hold our peace if you take legal steps showing your intention to leave your spouse unfilled and miserable permanently. But if you seek fulfillment and joy in another relationship, we'll have to take action against you.

The sequence needs to be reversed. The greatest emotional, social, moral, and spiritual damage comes at the point of marital breakdown—not when people try again.

The church should be mainly concerned with helping all couples understand, aspire to, and experience the joy that God wants for us in marriage. We should work to heal broken relationships, rather than passively letting them slide toward divorce.

We certainly should be concerned about biblical principles concerning remarriage. But we must make sure that we place our greatest emphasis at the right point in the priority list. What I'm saying doesn't necessitate changes in Adventist doctrine or in church policy. It merely reflects an observation Christ made in Matthew 23:23—about being so busy with what needs to be done that we ignore the even more important matters.

There's more than one way to strain at a gnat and swallow a camel.

FACTS AND FABLES

So Different, Yet So Alike

During the days that followed the deaths of Princess Diana and Mother Teresa—both of whom died the same week—the media worked overtime to report and comment on the impact of these two highly influential women.

The contrasts between the two are dramatic. One was cut down in the prime of life; the other died in old age. One was surrounded by glitz and glamour; the other was committed to asceticism. One's moral frailties and personal struggles were public knowledge; the other was a paragon of virtue and serenity.

Princess Diana's impact was made possible by youthfulness, beauty, the good fortune of marrying a prince, and—ironically—media that made her the most-photographed and most-discussed woman in the world. By contrast, a lifetime of personal piety and an unwavering commitment to spiritual values propelled Mother Teresa into the public eye.

I first learned from a talk-radio program that Mother Teresa had died. A question was being debated: Who was the better woman? The problem is, as Aristotle noted millennia ago, those who would find the right answer must first ask the right question.

Granted, most people more readily recognize virtue when it's clothed in asceticism and piety than when it comes in the garb of glamour. But the real question is How did each woman utilize the circumstances in which she found herself to promote the principles she believed in? How did each, in her own unique way, labor to make the world a better place? In answering these questions, we discover that the women had major similarities in addition to their many differences.

One lived in self-imposed poverty, the other in a palace. But both focused on those less fortunate.

One had the gnarled hands of the laborer; the other's reflected the ultimate in manicure. But both were willing to soil their hands for the good of others.

One's name was synonymous with prayer, the other's with pomp and ceremony. But both sought to bring hope where before there had been only despair.

One worked through church and religion, the other through government and high society. But both were committed to the uplifting of humanity.

In Matthew 25 Jesus says that God's true children are those about whom God can say: "I was hungry and you gave me something to eat, I was thirsty and you gave me something to drink, I was a stranger and you invited me in, I needed clothes and you clothed me, I was sick and you looked after me, I was in prison and you came to visit me" (verses 35, 36, NIV).

Despite their differences, both women appear to have met Jesus' criteria.

We needn't seek to become a carbon copy of either Princess Diana or Mother Teresa; we should simply be ourselves, as they were. Whatever our circumstances, and whether we reach out on a global or local scale, we can show genuine love and compassion for others. And as they both did, we can commit ourselves to making this world a better place because we were here.

FACTS AND FABLES

Sometimes We Just Don't Get It

First, the disclaimer: What I'm about to say isn't for atheists and agnostics—although they're welcome to listen in. My comments are for believers. Christians. Jews. Muslims. Those sorts.

Now some facts: I'm a Christian. A preacher. But, surprisingly, I'm not altogether happy about some of the ways God's name has crept into public discourse since September 11. Let me explain.

As the dust of devastation settles, heartening accounts of survival continue to emerge. Traffic jams, family interruptions, even the decision to buy a bagel—all are part of the saga of lives spared.

Then there's the other side. People at a new job for the first day, security officials incorrectly announcing that a building is safe, police and firefighters just doing their jobs—all are part of the saga of lives lost.

So when I hear the survivors praise God for looking out for them, I cringe on behalf of those to whom fate dealt a different hand. If God put it into the mind of one person to buy a bagel, couldn't He have put it into the minds of airport guards to detain the bearers of box cutters?

In our gratitude to be alive, and in our desire to give God the glory, we too often fail to consider the implications of what we're saying.

In my denomination we have a fund-raising program we call Investment. The concept is simple: A person commits to God the income from some venture, inviting Him to bless it.

Back in the mid-1980s, a man promised God he would give 25 cents for every extra shave he got from his Bic disposable. To his amazement, he began getting 80 and 90 shaves instead of his usual four or five. Other men from his church joined in, with similar results.

At the time, I was an editor for a denominational magazine. We thought the story inspiring and published it. On the cover we featured the participants—all lathered up and holding aloft their razors. What a miracle.

But the readers didn't all share our enthusiasm. One poignant letter went something like this: Yesterday a young mother of three learned she had terminal cancer. Yesterday a little boy chased a ball into the street and was killed. Yesterday millions went to bed hungry. And where was God during all this? He was busy sharpening Bic razors.

How do I explain the sharp-razor phenomenon now? I can't. There are some things for which satisfactory explanations elude us. But I do know that such stories, when viewed in the broader context of world suffering, not only add to the pain of those who already suffer, but raise disturbing questions about the character of God.

There are times when the most appropriate response—for the sake of our fellow humans and even God—is to simply be grateful for any good that comes our way and to refrain from opining about ultimate causes.

SCRIPTURE RECONSIDERED

A Definition of Sin

Theologians spend a lot of time talking about sin. Is sin a state of being, or is it an action? Is it both? Or perhaps neither?

Does sin separate us from God? Or does separation from God result in sin? Or are separation and sin combined in a vicious downward spiral? Do we sin because we're sinners? Or are we sinners because we sin?

Before long our arguments can resemble the classic—but ultimately unhelpful— question: which came first, the chicken or the egg?

Now don't get me wrong. I don't wish in any way to undercut the necessity of sound theology. It's important that we have clear understandings of what the Bible actually teaches about such topics. They have crucial implications.

But in the same way that the scientific description of a kiss falls far short of the actual experience, clinically accurate theological definitions can be far removed from our everyday lives.

As a child, I used to think of sin as behavior that caused God to be upset with me. God had drawn up laws to test my allegiance. When I transgressed them, I incurred His displeasure, and He would refuse to deal with me until I'd adequately sought forgiveness. To me, God's expectations were quite arbitrary.

Fortunately, I no longer view God or His laws in that way—in part, because I no longer use only the analogy of judicial law to try to understand what God's law is all about.

In our legal system laws are arbitrary—at least to some degree. And so are punishments. True, they theoretically are for our good. But often it is questionable whether they really are.

Furthermore, whether the speed limit is 50 miles per hour or 60 miles per hour is quite subjective. And whether the penalty for an infraction should be a $25 fine or a $250 fine is equally subjective.

On the other hand, scientific laws—such as the law of gravity—represent a totally different concept of law. These laws describe rather than prescribe. In the natural world we don't talk about reward and punishment; we talk about consequence—cause and effect. An unrestrained rock doesn't plummet to avoid punishment. It falls because of certain properties inherent in the universe's makeup.

Similarly, I believe that God's laws are not arbitrary rules of governance. Rather, they're factual statements about how we must function if we're to be what God designed us to be. Granted the nature of our design, the course God advocates is the only sensible one. It's the only course that won't, in the long run, be self-destructive.

I like the way J. B. Phillips translates Paul's admonition: "With eyes wide open to the mercies of God, I beg you, my brothers, as an act of intelligent worship, to give him your bodies, as a living sacrifice, consecrated to him and acceptable by him" (Romans 12:1, Phillips).

Following God's way is simply the *intelligent* thing do. It is living the life for which God, the Designer, designed us. It is learning to experience and appreciate now the kind of life that we must live if we are to survive for eternity.

In this context my personal working definition of sin—and please don't try to strain it through too fine a theological sieve, because it has its inadequacies—is that sin is anything less than the best.

God has great expectations for His children. We're "fearfully and wonderfully made" (Psalm 139:14). "Eye hath not seen, nor ear heard" the wonderful things that He has in mind for redeemed humanity (1 Corinthians 2:9). It's our responsibility to experience life to the full—now and forever.

In all aspects of our lives—human relations, the Sabbath, healthful living, simplicity of lifestyle, care and concern for others, developing a relationship with Christ, whatever—God doesn't want us to settle for less than the best. And I find it easy to relate to a God who wants that kind of fulfillment for His creatures.

SCRIPTURE RECONSIDERED

A Great Story

I like success stories. And 2 Chronicles 20 contains one of the best. Further, I believe it's instructive for us today. So let's note just a few points.

Contrary to a belief that's popular in some circles these days, followers of God aren't guaranteed a trouble-free existence. In fact, the Bible repeatedly describes how some of God's greatest followers faced the most trying circumstances. For example, in the 2 Chronicles 20 story, a vast army is bearing down on "good king" Jehoshaphat.

Equally false is the belief that God's true followers never experience fear, perplexity, or discouragement. Followers of God are still human. They're not without emotion. So Jehoshaphat is "badly shaken" (verse 3, TLB) by the news of the approaching enemy.

But despite the difficulties that come, and despite their fears and concerns, true followers of God know where their source of strength lies. Thus Jehoshaphat calls all the people together to plead unitedly to God for deliverance. They recognize that if they are to survive this threat, it will be because of God's involvement, not because of their own strength.

"O our God, won't you stop them?" they call out in anguish. "We have no way to protect ourselves against this mighty army. We don't know what to do, but we are looking to you" (verse 12, TLB).

Only when humans fully realize their inadequacy and reach out earnestly to God can He work as dramatically as He would like. However—and we as humans don't understand why—God often doesn't participate as we feel He should. But in this story God *does* participate. His Spirit falls upon one of the men, who delivers a special message for the people:

"Listen to me, all you people of Judah and Jerusalem, and you, O king Jehoshaphat!" the man exclaims. "The Lord says, 'Don't be afraid! Don't be paralyzed by this mighty army! For the battle is not yours, but God's! Tomorrow, go down and attack them! . . . But you will not need to fight! Take your places; stand quietly and see the incredible rescue operation God will perform for you, O people of Judah and Jerusalem! Don't be afraid or discouraged! Go out there tomorrow, for the Lord is with you!' " (verses 15-17, TLB).

Too often we forget that we don't have to slug it out with the devil blow for blow. The battle is God's. The challenge for us is to want Him to fight on our behalf, to put our will on His side, to have the faith to proceed even when the way seems dark.

Fortunately, in the story of Jehoshaphat, the people have that kind of faith. In fact, so great is their faith that they hold a praise service even before they've seen the prediction become a reality.

"Listen to me, O people of Judah and Jerusalem," Jehoshaphat tells the army as it makes its way out to meet the enemy. "Believe in the Lord your God, and you shall have success! Believe his prophets, and everything will be all right!" (verse 20, TLB). Then, after consultation, the Jewish leaders decide that a choir should lead the army, singing praises to God for the victory that He is about to give them.

As the choir begins to sing, it so rocks the enemy soldiers that they begin to kill each other. In fact, *not one* enemy escapes. And so great is the plunder the Jews find on the battlefield that it takes three days to cart it all away.

Now, I'm not sure how to determine just when faith ceases and presumption begins. (I imagine that if I had been in the choir as it marched out of Jerusalem, I'd have suggested that it might be wise for the soldiers to go first.)

Further, I'm not always sure just how to translate the principles of what happened thousands of years ago into the context in which you and I find ourselves today. How much should we do, and how much should we let Him do?

But one thing I'm certain of: If we find the proper balance, and if we let God accomplish through us what He wants to accomplish, the reaction of onlookers will be the same as it was back then: "When the surrounding kingdoms heard that the Lord himself had fought against the enemies of Israel, the fear of God fell upon them" (verse 29, TLB).

SCRIPTURE RECONSIDERED

A Story Revisited

You know the story. The woman was caught in adultery—red-handed.

She was dragged unceremoniously to Jesus, who was questioned about how she should be dealt with. He said the criterion for throwing the book (i.e., stones) at her was to be without sin. When everyone slunk away, Jesus told the woman He didn't condemn her, despite what she'd done. But He did recommend major behavior modification. She went home to ponder what He'd said. And He began another day of ministry. End of story.

Well, not quite. At least I can imagine it wasn't.

You see, a church board meeting was scheduled for that night. And a good many of the people who were present at the early-morning confrontation were also members of the board. They may not have had much to say to Jesus, but they had a lot they wanted to say to the board.

The chair's devotional thought for the evening focused on the urgent need not only to obey God but to take a strong stand against disobedience. He reminded those present of the clear statements of Scripture concerning the penalty for inappropriate behavior.

Adultery was worthy of death (Leviticus 20:10). So was human sacrifice (Leviticus 20:2), having a familiar spirit (Leviticus 20:27), blasphemy (Leviticus 24:16), Sabbathbreaking (Numbers 15:32-36), serving false gods (Deuteronomy 13:6-11; 17:2-5), and incorrigibility (Deuteronomy 22:13-21). And these were but a few examples he'd gleaned from a quick perusal of only three books.

"I know there are some in the church these days who continually emphasize compassion," he said. "But if God had wanted these cases treated with compassion, He certainly wouldn't have given Moses the instruction that we read in the passages I've cited."

After prayer and the approval of the previous meeting's minutes, the chair led the board into a discussion of what had happened that morning—even though it wasn't on the agenda that had been mailed a few days before to the board members. The discussion centered on whether or not the response given at the early-morning confrontation was adequate. Did more decisive action need to be taken?

"I recognize that the case is complicated," said one woman. "As we all know, the offender's background isn't ideal. She has had some bad breaks in life. But I don't see how we can allow blatant sin to go unpunished. Either we follow the teachings of Scripture, or we don't. Wrong is wrong, and that's that."

"I too am somewhat sympathetic toward the offender," said another board member. "She has faced a number of disadvantages. And I think it fair to say that some people have taken advantage of her. However, circumstances are no excuse for sin. What she did was wrong—totally wrong. Further, it's public knowledge. If we don't mete out the prescribed penalty, the fair name of the church will be sullied. I don't like having to do it, but I see no other option."

"I think that's the crucial point—that it *is* public knowledge," said another speaker. "We have to remember that our young people are very quick to spot hypocrisy and double standards. If we turn a blind eye to what this woman has done, they're going to say that we're soft on sin. And they'll use it as an excuse to do whatever they want. Out of concern for our youth, we have to take a strong stand on this case."

"Some of you seem to be implying that we have a choice in what we do," said another board member, waving a little black book. "But we don't. It says right here in the church manual that even if the person is repentant, we still have an obligation to demonstrate our abhorrence of what has been done. We must make a public statement by our response. If we don't, not only are we ignoring the teaching of Scripture; we're ignoring the church manual. That would be setting a dangerous precedent."

The discussion went on for some time, but few new arguments came forth. Everyone agreed that mercy had its place—but so did justice and protecting the fair name of the church.

When the vote was taken, it wasn't unanimous, but it was convincing: The woman should be stoned. The chair said he would announce the time and place at church that coming Sabbath.

When word of the board's decision reached Jesus, He merely bowed His head and said, "Father, forgive them, for they know not what they do."

SCRIPTURE RECONSIDERED

A Story Revisited—Again

In "A Story Revisited" we took a look at the story of the woman caught in adultery—the one to whom Jesus said, "Neither do I condemn thee: go, and sin no more" (John 8:11).

In a flight of imagination I suggested that at a church board meeting that night Jesus' action was reversed—that it was decided that she definitely should be stoned: to demonstrate the church's abhorrence of sin, to maintain the fair name of the church, to honor the provisions of the church manual, and to keep the youth from accusing church leaders of hypocrisy and double standards.

So the execution was carried out, and the woman was buried in the section of the local cemetery reserved for those with no denominational affiliation. (She had been officially disfellowshipped before the stoning.) And before many weeks passed, the incident was forgotten.

Then one Sabbath a woman wearing garish clothes and lots of cheap jewelry walked into the church and took a seat near the back. Her overdose of perfume failed to hide the smell of stale tobacco. And her makeup couldn't mask the deep lines on her face. Not a few members of the congregation craned their necks for a better look.

During the personal ministries period one of the church members was telling about his outreach and how he was endeavoring to share truth with those in darkness.

Suddenly the garishly dressed, cheaply bejeweled woman broke into sobs. "Excuse me," she blurted out, standing to her feet, "but I must find this truth you're talking about. I *have* to find it."

One of the church elders ushered her into the pastor's study, and her whole sordid story burst forth. She was a prostitute. Had been since she became a mainline drug user at the age of 12. Life for her was sheer hell, and she simply had to find a way of escape. She was desperate.

The elder called his wife. And when his wife heard the horrors to which the woman had been subjected, she put her arms around her and invited her to come to their home. She didn't even seem to notice the smell of tobacco or the heavy makeup that dripped onto her nice Sabbath dress as the poor woman cried.

Three weeks later during the personal ministries period, the elder and his wife told the story. Then the prostitute stood up to testify. She told how in those three weeks she had gone off drugs. For the first time in her life she had hope.

There wasn't a dry eye as people listened to her describe what she'd been and how God, working through human love, had transformed her almost overnight.

From that day church members phoned her regularly to see how she was faring. Every Sabbath she was invited out for lunch. One church member provided an apartment—rent-free. Another all but gave her a car. Another offered her a job. Never had she been so well treated. She was overwhelmed.

And it wasn't just the local congregation. Other congregations invited her to speak at youth meetings, for women's prayer groups, for church services. And at camp meeting she stood up before 5,000 people and for 30 minutes described the depths to which she'd fallen and the heights to which she'd risen, thanks to the power of God and the help of her church friends.

One day the transformed prostitute invited a church friend to accompany her to the funeral of a prostitute who used to work the streets with her. The dead woman had overdosed.

They watched as the prostitute's unadorned coffin was slowly lowered into the ground in the section of the cemetery for those with no denominational affiliation. But as they turned to go, a grave that still wasn't grassed over caught the attention of the now-transformed woman of the street. She stepped closer to see the name on the plain headstone.

"I've met that woman!" she exclaimed. "In a pub a few months ago. She told me she was going to be stoned the next day by her church because she'd committed adultery. But wait! I'm sure she said it was *our* church that was doing it!"

Reluctantly, painfully, the church member acknowledged what had happened. Yes, the church had stoned the woman.

When it was all out, the newly converted former prostitute slumped onto the not-yet-grassed-over grave and, with tears streaming down her face, cried out, "O God, thank You that I fell into sin *before* finding the church rather than *after.*"

SCRIPTURE RECONSIDERED

Flat Tires and Other Miracles

When a flat tire kept Domingo Pacheco from boarding ValuJet's doomed Flight 592 on May 11, 1996, his mother declared, "It's God's way of saying you weren't supposed to be on that flight."

Pacheco lived because of a flat tire. One hundred nine others had no tire trouble and died. Pacheco's family sings God's praises for His intervention. The families of the 109 passengers without car trouble wrestle with the question: How could God allow such a terrible tragedy?

Why is it that we go through life with scarcely a mention of God—yet give us a narrow escape from tragedy, and even the most secular among us suddenly bring God into the picture?

Hundreds of people miss flights every day because of flat tires, traffic jams, and a host of other disruptions. We don't view these failures to be on time as God-ordained. But let a plane crash, and a delay suddenly assumes the status of a miracle.

I'm a member of the clergy. I believe in God and spend a lot of time talking about Him. I also spend a lot of time trying to comfort grieving people. And I find that much of the talk about God that feels so good for a fortunate few actually intensifies the pain of those not so fortunate.

If God could save Domingo Pacheco by flattening his tire, couldn't He also have flattened dozens of other tires? Were the others less worthy of God's help? less important in His overall scheme?

Ironically, the seeming goodness of God in sparing one person's life dramatically heightens the seeming callousness of God in failing to spare others. Crediting God with narrow escapes makes those whose loved ones didn't escape feel abandoned by God. But it also can set up the fortunate ones for greater spiritual anguish later on.

If God gets the credit for miraculously saving someone from certain death now, who is going to get the blame if one month from now that same person discovers that he or she has a terminal illness? Either it comes from God—be it good or bad—or it doesn't. We can't have it both ways.

Understandably, we want to believe that the universe makes total sense and that God always rewards good people. Yet the Bible says: "The race is not to the swift or the battle to the strong, nor does food come to the wise or wealth to the brilliant or favor to the learned; but time and chance happen to them all" (Ecclesiastes 9:11, NIV).

If King Solomon felt uncomfortable with the seeming unfairness of life's outcomes, then surely we should be cautious lest we read too much about God's will into the events that transpire around us—be they to our advantage or to our disadvantage.

Whether or not events turn out the way we want probably tells us little about God's involvement. Even the Bible acknowledges that "time and chance" play a major role in life—and probably in death, too.

SCRIPTURE RECONSIDERED

From Rags to Riches

It's a rather remarkable story. I heard the first part many years ago. But I hadn't heard the ending—which is even more amazing—until recently during a sermon on stewardship.

You know the story. A woman in rags, with perhaps several little waifs clutching at her robe, slinks into the Temple. She glances around to make sure no one is looking, and gently drops two mites into the offering receptacle. She then retreats, always looking at the ground lest anyone see the humiliation in her eyes. But what she has done doesn't go unnoticed in heaven.

Because stewardship is based on the principle of "you can't outgive God"—"You shovel into God's bin with your little shovel, and He shovels back into your bin with His big shovel" is how the preacher described it—the woman goes home from the Temple and waits to see what will happen. She isn't disappointed.

That week she picks up two new laundry customers. And when she next goes to the Temple, she's able to give four mites and doesn't hang her head quite so much.

Now there's no holding her back. She understands the principle: the more you give, the more you get. Soon she can't do all the laundry that's coming her way. She hires the widow next door. Then she hires another. Now when she goes to the Temple she deposits a small bag of money in the treasury rather than a few measly coins. She only wishes she had discovered the principle sooner.

With so much money at her disposal, the fact that she's a widow and has several small children no longer proves the romantic obstacle it once was. Soon a wealthy neighbor proposes, they marry, give ever-greater offerings, and live happily ever after.

OK. I admit it. The preacher didn't actually say all that. I simply took what he was saying, and let my mind wander a bit, and the story emerged. But I'm being absolutely true to his thesis in applying it as I have.

He made many sweeping statements with few qualifications. And in doing so, I think he failed to present the truth about tithes and offerings. And his isn't the first such discourse I've heard on the topic.

What I'm saying is that, while we must never understate the blessing that comes from tithing and freewill giving, we also must not overstate the case. I believe every person is blessed for giving. But that blessing doesn't always come in monetary form. It may be good health. It may be the peace of mind of knowing that we have a Father in heaven. It may be the joy of being partners with God. It may be a happy home. Or it may be material prosperity.

While it's true that the Bible talks about the blessings—crops protected from pests, good yields, an enviable standard of living (Malachi 3:10-12)—it also says we'll have the poor with us always (John 12:8). And Jesus didn't say we would have them only until they all learned the principles of stewardship.

True, we can cite many wonderful examples of people's crops being miraculously protected from storm or pests. But we can cite numerous other examples in which the crops of equally devout tithe payers are destroyed. It's a paradox, a mystery.

Quite frankly, I imagine that the widow in the biblical story never saw any significant change in her financial status. I doubt that she ever gave much more than two mites, and there may have been times when she didn't have even that. But I'm sure that she felt tremendously blessed by God—because she had never fallen victim to the heresy, too often promoted today, that tithing guarantees smooth passage from rags to riches.

SCRIPTURE RECONSIDERED

Harmonizing the Old and New

When I read the Gospel of John and compare it with, say, the book of Judges, I must admit that I sometimes wonder if I'm reading about the same God. And I don't think I'm alone in my reaction.

In fact, one could get the impression that even Jesus tried to distance Himself from some of the barbaric laws introduced during the time of Moses. But did He really?

In the first few verses of Matthew 19 we read a discussion between Jesus and the Pharisees concerning divorce. They point out that Moses required only that a man give his wife a bill of divorcement if he wished to terminate his marriage. In contrast, Jesus contends that a marriage can be dissolved only if there's unfaithfulness.

To the casual observer, it might seem that Jesus' teaching shows concern for the rights and feelings of women, while Moses' teaching shows none at all. But such isn't the case.

In the time of Moses, men "divorced" their wives simply because they didn't like the way a woman might herd the sheep, build the campfire, snore at night, or be incapable of having more than about one baby each year.

No man wanted to marry a woman who had been rejected, for there was no guaranteeing that her husband wouldn't change his mind after a week, month, year, or decade and want her back. Then sparks would fly. And the new husband would have no legal ground to keep her, as she was technically still the wife of the first husband.

As a result, "divorced" women were social outcasts who often became slaves or prostitutes simply to survive. It was a grim situation. But Moses' requirement that rejected wives be given a bill of divorcement gave women legal standing. And with that standing came the possibility of remarriage and a decent life, despite having been rejected.

Or take the "an eye for an eye, and a tooth for a tooth" regulation of Moses' day (see Exodus 21:24). It was harsh, certainly. But it was nowhere near as harsh as the way people often reacted when they had a grievance. The most inconsequential act against someone else could open the floodgates of vengeance, and offenders seldom lived to make the same mistake again.

Given this cultural context, when Moses told the Hebrews they must limit their retaliation to "an eye for an eye, and a tooth for a tooth," it probably caused just as much amazement as when Jesus told His listeners that they should love their enemies. In each case the course advocated seemed so unreasonably passive, so out of character with what the people were used to.

Similarly, God's command that the Israelites totally annihilate certain of their enemies—killing men, women, children, and even cattle—may reveal more kindness than we traditionally have perceived.

In those days conquering nations committed atrocities against the vanquished that would make death seem a welcome escape. While genocide seems ruthless to us, it may have been considerably less cruel treatment than Israel's opponents would have received had God not laid down the guidelines He did.

While I don't completely understand the reasons behind much of what's recorded in the Old Testament, I believe that many things we view as barbaric today were in fact a great revelation of love.

Put another way, were we to draw a line on a graph intersecting point A (what the Hebrews would have been like without Moses' commands) and point B (what they were as a result of his commands), I think the line would also intersect point C (what Jesus taught while He was here on earth).

God can't take anyone in just one step from the pit of sin to where He wants them. Not even you or me.

SCRIPTURE RECONSIDERED

Let's Be for Real

This essay is about sanctification.

For some Adventists the word is associated with legalism. With do's and don'ts. With checklists.

For me, it's good news. And to a great degree I can thank one of my former college teachers for my attitude.

This particular teacher had the unique ability of examining old truths in new terms of reference. Shunning theological jargon, he tried to describe the essence of an experience in terms understandable to everyone. By his definition, sanctification was the process of becoming "authentically human."

In Eden, God created Adam and Eve "in his own image" (Genesis 1:27). These beings, as they came from the hand of God, were capable of the fullest enjoyment of all their faculties. They communed with God—mind with mind, heart with heart, spirit with spirit. Except by their own choice, there was no limit to the possibilities of their development. They were authentic humanity. *Real* people.

Abusing their power of choice and choosing to be something other than what they'd been created to be, they became something far less. We see them clutching furtively at a few fig leaves, trying to cover their nakedness. Sin had reduced God's ultimate creation to a subhuman existence. A major component now was missing.

A piece of perceptive doggerel describes it well: "I turned to speak to God about the world's despair; but to make bad matters worse, I found God wasn't there. God turned to speak to me—don't anybody laugh; God found I wasn't there—at least, not over half."

But God didn't reject humanity because of sin. He loved and forgave. And He does even more than that.

Says Ellen White: "God's forgiveness is not merely a judicial act by which He sets us free from condemnation. It is not only forgiveness *for* sin, but reclaiming *from* sin" (*Thoughts From the Mount of Blessing,* p. 114).

"In the beginning God created man in His own likeness. . . . His mind was well balanced, and all the powers of his being were harmonious. . . . It was to restore this that the plan of salvation was devised. . . . To bring him back to the perfection in which he was first created is the great object of life—the object that underlies every other" (*Patriarchs and Prophets,* p. 595).

"The central theme of the Bible, the theme about which every other in the whole book clusters, is the redemption plan, the restoration in the human soul of the image of God. . . . The burden of every book and every passage of the Bible is the unfolding of this wondrous theme, man's uplifting, the power of God, 'which giveth us the victory through our Lord Jesus Christ'" (*Education,* pp. 125, 126).

"To show what every human being might become; what, through the indwelling of humanity by divinity, all who received Him [Christ] would become—for this, Christ came to the world" (*Ibid.,* p. 74).

"Higher than the highest human thought can reach is God's ideal for His children" (*Ibid.,* p. 18).

Sanctification, then, isn't a method of earning one's way to heaven. Nor is it God's entrance exam, designed to eliminate most of heaven's candidates.

Sanctification is the process of learning to live the type of life for which we were designed, the type of life we'll live throughout eternity. It's a daily refusal to live a subhuman life. A determination to live the authentically human life.

It's a requirement, yes. But more than that, it's a high privilege. It isn't in contrast to the gospel; it's simply more of the same good news.

The Living Bible says in Romans 5:1, 2: "So now, since we have been made right in God's sight by faith in his promises, we can have real peace with him because of what Jesus Christ our Lord has done for us. . . . And we confidently and joyfully look forward to actually becoming all that God has had in mind for us to be."

That's sanctification.

SCRIPTURE RECONSIDERED

Off the Track?

If I'd been one of the disciples when Jesus told His parable about the sheep being separated from the goats at the end of the world (Matthew 25:31-46), I'm afraid I'd have protested—inwardly, at least.

In fact, I find it hard to believe that a person such as Peter wouldn't have objected and said, "Lord, I don't mean to be rude, but do You really mean what You just said? Are you sure that's the criteria for separating the saved from the lost?"

And I can imagine others chiming in: "Surely You meant to say that the saved will be those who've overcome every known sin in their lives. Those who've gained the victory over drinking and smoking and gambling and carousing. Those who no longer swear or tell off-color stories. Those who go to church every week and pay a second tithe. Those who keep the seventh-day Sabbath. Those who witness for the truth."

Or certainly someone such as John would have said, "Excuse me, Lord, but didn't You mean to say that the saved will be those with a correct understanding of salvation theology? those who don't seek righteousness by good deeds, but who accept God's free gift? Aren't the saved those who live totally by faith?"

But I wasn't there. And no one else seems to have taken Jesus to task for suggesting that the saved will be those who've taken more than a passing interest in the down-and-outers—the hungry, the thirsty, the strangers, the naked, the sick, the prisoners. But that's not all.

If I'd been the scribe when James dictated his little five-chapter letter, I'd have interjected when he gave his definition of "pure religion" (James 1:27).

"Pastor James," I'd have said, "if you're determined to define religion in terms of behavior—and thereby set yourself up to be called a legalist—couldn't you at least place personal piety ahead of social responsibility? If you put visiting the orphans and the widows ahead of keeping oneself unspotted from the world, you're preaching a social gospel."

And even Paul, despite his excellent discourses on the relationship of faith and works, falls into a similar trap: "Carry each other's burdens, and in this way you will fulfill the law of Christ" (Galatians 6:2, NIV). Now, surely Paul, of all people, would have realized that there's more to lawkeeping than just helping those in need.

So why were Jesus and James and Paul—to mention but a few of the Bible writers—so confused? The fact is, *they* weren't. *We* are.

Jesus said there are two great responsibilities: to God and to fellow humans. Both call on us to focus outside ourselves.

Salvation *is* the foundation on which all else must be built. But I believe that some of us have spent too much time concentrating on it to the neglect of our purpose for being here in this world.

For some it has been a legalistic concern about becoming good enough for God to accept. For others it has been an equally legalistic and often smug concern about developing sufficient theological astuteness to know that we can never become good enough to earn God's favor. But either way, the focus is on self.

Granted, we must never presume on God's goodness. But God has stated simply and unequivocally that if we accept His grace, we have salvation. We need to accept that salvation gratefully, thank God for it every day, and then get on with the task God has given us.

And if I read my Bible correctly, a major aspect of that task is working on behalf of those whose lives may not be as blessed as our own. And the Bible isn't speaking of spiritual poverty and spiritual malnutrition alone. It's also speaking of physical needs.

I believe we need to refocus our priorities. And when we do, we may discover that the needs are at our doorstep, and we've been too preoccupied with our own salvation to notice them.

SCRIPTURE RECONSIDERED

One Thing I Know

We live in an age of education. We worship at the feet of the degreed gurus whose research and study have provided wisdom so profound that the uneducated masses can only marvel. How could these modern-day Wise Men be wrong? After all, are they not men of science?

We live in an age of proof. Be it physics, chemistry, sociology, or theology, a position must be supported by the latest empirical evidence, or it's suspect.

We live in an age of skepticism. Functions of nature that for centuries were believed to reside exclusively in the domain of God are now being given scientific explanations. How much trust can be put in an old book of folklore when we live in an age of enlightenment?

We live in an age of cynicism. For, despite all our scientific advance, utopia hasn't emerged. We see strains of disease that are now becoming immune to our wonder drugs. Sociology and psychology haven't removed personal anxiety. And the threat of nuclear war hangs over our heads.

We live in an age when it's becoming increasingly difficult to express faith in a Creator-Sustainer-Redeemer God and still retain one's credibility. What could the average person know about such ultimate realities? Why, even the theologians can't agree.

And that's why the story found in John 9 is so refreshing. In this chapter we read about a man born blind who was healed by Jesus. Contrary to what one might expect, the leaders of the day weren't rejoicing over the man's good fortune—for Jesus' action in healing the man ran counter to certain theological presuppositions of the day.

The man ultimately was brought before the Jewish leaders for questioning. Did he know who had healed him? Did he know that the man who had healed him was purported to be a sinner? Did he recognize the theological implications of being healed by such a man?

Here was an ordinary uneducated man, standing before the learned men of his day, being questioned about a phenomenal experience he'd just had, concerning which his questioners were skeptical.

He didn't fully appreciate their reasons for skepticism, let alone the theological implications to which they alluded. So he simply told them what he did understand. "Whether he be a sinner or no, I know not: one thing I know, that, whereas I was blind, now I see" (John 9:25).

Those few simple words from uneducated lips constitute one of the most eloquent testimonies to God ever given. There had come into that man's life a change—a change that he didn't fully understand, but that had turned his life around completely. Darkness had turned into day. It had happened because of his contact with a man called Jesus. And none of his listeners could gainsay such a testimony.

Most of us today don't have the educational background nor the skills necessary to enter into debate with the learned and the skeptical. But each of us should be able to share the testimony of the man of John 9. "Whether the transformation wrought in my life by the Holy Spirit be scientifically explicable or not, I can't say. But this I do know: My life has been totally changed."

To recognize the eloquence of such a testimony is not to encourage an illogical or simplistic religion. Nor is it to advocate that we not engage in higher academic pursuits. It's merely a recognition that the testimony of a few simple but heartfelt words can be just as powerful, and just as great an honor to God, as a multitude of complex phrases from the learned.

Indeed, until we can each give the simple testimony "I once was blind, but now I see," all our well-worded phrases will be in vain.

LIVING IN A MIXED-UP WORLD

Can We Really Afford It?

Excuse my cynicism, but I don't have a lot of faith in President George W. Bush's faith-based initiative. Either God or the government is going to get short shrift. And it may be both.

For starters, the government doesn't—and shouldn't—hand out money willy-nilly. There are always strings attached. And the strings aren't merely matters of procedure. Often they derive from social and moral values.

A case in point: Bush has declared that overseas family-planning programs can wave bye-bye to U.S. funding if their counseling presents abortion as an option. So how will the president relate to those *faith-based* organizations that present the possibility of abortion?

Are all faith-based entities equal in the eyes of the people who participate in the opinion polls that drive the politicians who make the laws?

I doubt it.

For instance, how many Americans would want the Church of Satan to be a government-funded distributor of charity? And what about those cults accused of brainwashing? If you've just spent a few thousand dollars to get your kid deprogrammed, do you want the government handing the offending group a few million dollars to aid in its humanitarian work? Would an atheist organization qualify as a faith-based entity?

After all, both atheism and theism require faith.

Inevitably the government will have to draw the line concerning who qualifies as a faith-based organization. And it doesn't take a prophet to predict that (1) the organizations receiving the governmental thumbs-down aren't going to take it well; and (2) attorneys are going to relish the myriad court challenges that will be filed.

Sadder still, a lot of faith-based organizations are going to lose sight of their real raison d'être and make whatever compromises are necessary to win Uncle Sam's money.

But we've looked at only part of the picture. The reality is, the driving force behind almost every church activity is the retaining or gaining of adherents. The seemingly secular activities are, I would suggest, bridge-builders to put church members in touch with nonmembers, to break down prejudice and to get names, addresses, and phone numbers of potential members.

Only in theory can the spiritual and secular ministries of faith-based entities be separated. In reality, they're so intertwined that government financing of one is inevitably financing of the other.

Which means that every recipient is spiritually advantaged, and every nonrecipient is spiritually disadvantaged. And that takes us perilously close to violating the First Amendment's establishment clause.

The church where I'm pastor could certainly benefit from having a few million dollars pass through its hands. And it might even save the government some money.

I'm just not so sure our democracy could afford it.

LIVING IN A MIXED-UP WORLD

Don't Forget the Present

The eighteenth-century English poet Alexander Pope, in lines often lifted from context—as I'm doing to a degree here—states: "Hope springs eternal in the human breast: Man never is, but always to be blest."

Demonstrating the validity of Pope's words, a great many people in today's society—Adventists included—are bartering the present for the future. Children are born, they learn to walk and talk, they go to school, they pass through the beautiful metamorphosis of childhood. Yet fathers, and often mothers, are too busy getting an education, climbing the corporate ladder, establishing a career, and becoming financially secure to experience the ecstasy that accompanies interaction with those young lives.

When the parents' goals are achieved (if they ever are), they often prove less satisfying than envisioned. At the same time, events forever gone but not fully savored take on new significance. But they remain forever irretrievable.

Adventists, particularly in North America, are an upwardly mobile segment of society. We also are a driven people, success-conscious. Our emphasis on education and our sense of mission contribute to this phenomenon. While such characteristics are commendable, they also open the door to serious pitfalls. Imbalance, intemperance, and inverted priorities are a danger even in the pursuit of worthwhile goals.

In a book entitled *I'd Pick More Daisies* Betty Holbrook shares a statement from Frank Dickey. This statement was her source for the book's title: "If had my life to live over, I would relax more. I wouldn't take so many things so seriously. . . . I would climb more mountains, and swim more rivers. . . . I'd start barefooted earlier in the spring and stay that way until later in the fall. . . . I'd pick more daisies!"

Don't Forget the Present

How many of us take time to become well acquainted with our neighbors? How many of us take time to write letters to loved ones, to remember special events in the lives of others, simply to sit and watch the heavenly fireworks of a spring storm or savor the smell of the earth when the storm has ended? Or are we reserving such experiences until after the house is completed, the dissertation written, the corporate merger finalized, the crops planted, the church building project finished?

While we need to plan for the future and always live the present in such a manner that we safeguard future happiness, we must avoid sacrificing the present for the future. We have no guarantee that our lives will continue beyond the present moment. "Tomorrow never comes" may prove more than a truism.

Life doesn't begin with the achievement of some future goal or the arrival at some higher plateau; life is in the here and now.

The crucial danger against which we must contend is, as one writer has noted, not that life shall end; rather, that life shall never truly have begun.

LIVING IN A MIXED-UP WORLD

Face It, It's a Faith Issue

Some time ago I read a news report claiming that at the Scopes monkey trial, the loser won. I suggest that everyone lost—because the exercise perpetuated the myth that it's possible to know empirically how life forms originated.

The writer stated: "Scientists agree about the validity of the theory of evolution that all organisms evolved from a common ancestor through a process of natural selection."

I disagree.

Not all *evolutionists,* let alone all *scientists,* believe that assertion. In fact, the theory of evolution has become increasingly fragmented during the past few decades since 1960, when evolutionist G. A. Kerkut, then a professor of physiology and biochemistry at the University of Southampton in England, wrote the book *Implications of Evolution.*

Kerkut stated: "The theory of evolution as presented by orthodox evolutionists is in many ways a satisfying explanation of some of the evidence. At the same time I think that the attempt to explain all living forms in terms of an evolution *from a unique source,* though a brave and valid attempt, is one that is premature and not satisfactorily supported by present-day evidence."

He argued that orthodox evolution is based on seven assumptions that "by their nature are not capable of experimental verification." Even if it were possible to mimic in today's laboratories the events that are assumed to have happened, "all it shows is that it is *possible* for such a change to take place." It doesn't prove the events did take place.

Granted, I'm a creationist. However, I readily admit that creationist models fail to answer myriad questions adequately. For example, if only a few thousand years ago God created a world where lions grazed with cattle, how do we explain the tooth structure (for flesh-tearing), musculature (for pouncing on prey), and the digestive system (definitely carnivorous) of lions today?

But do evolutionist models fare any better? Take sexual reproduction, for instance. As the theory goes, inert matter sprang to life. Single-cell self-replicating organisms became multicell self-replicating organisms/creatures.

At some point one line of creatures began to develop a nonessential protrusion, while another line developed a nonessential indentation. With the passage of time the nonessential protrusion developed into a conduit for nonessential sperm. Simultaneously, the nonessential indentation developed a womb to receive a nonessential egg. Yet throughout, both lines remained self-replicating.

Then one day the two lines of creatures chanced to discover the pleasurable complement of the protrusion and indentation—and self-replication became a thing of the past!

Keep in mind, however, that the interdependence of sexual reproduction actually placed the creatures at greater risk—because if the creature could find no partner, there was no offspring and no survival.

So why this commentary?

For the same reason the evolutionist Kerkut wrote his book: "It will have succeeded in its task if it . . . brings back to light many assumptions tidily packaged and put away as being no longer open to question."

LIVING IN A MIXED-UP WORLD

For the Term of His Natural Life

The sentence: banishment . . . for life.

No, it's not the year 1800. The court isn't sitting in merry old England. The criminal hasn't stolen a loaf of bread. He won't be transported to Australia's infamous Botany Bay or Port Arthur. And Australian writer Marcus Clark won't be chronicling his plight. But for one 22-year-old, it's over. The tribunal has ruled.

And what heinous crime has this young man committed? Just why has he received what's thought to be the harshest sentence—actually, it's life *plus* three years—ever handed down?

He hasn't played according to the rules—of football!

According to the newspaper report, the Mornington Peninsula Football League tribunal (in Australia) suspended Gary Dyer from playing football for life "plus three years" when he was found guilty of hitting, head-butting, and spitting at an umpire recently.

"He was banned for life for elbowing one field umpire, two years for head-butting the other field umpire, and one year for spitting on a field and boundary umpire," the report said.

In addition to the umpire-related bookings, Dyer faced charges "for striking and unduly rough play involving opposition players."

Quite frankly, I don't know a lot about football—particularly the kind played in Australia. And I don't know if the penalties the tribunal handed down are justified. Nor do I know whether Mr. Dyer is actually guilty of the offenses for which he was convicted. But I find myself sympathizing with the tribunal—because I think they were trying to make a statement about the growing need for respect for authority.

While the emphasis on individual freedom that came out of the

1960s has in many ways produced a positive change, it at times has caused us to lose respect for legitimate authority. I once worked with a man who repeatedly said: "The boss may not always be right, but he's *always* the boss."

These days, however, the attitude seems to prevail that we should be subject to authority only so long as it harmonizes with what we want. But let someone in authority go against our wishes, and we may see a touch of Gary Dyer emerging.

I'm not suggesting that we should sit back and suffer abuse from those who would lord it over us. I think it quite reasonable to try to make a situation better or to try to remove oneself from the situation altogether.

But if our society is to lay legitimate claim to being civilized, there are times we must push our own desires and wishes into the background and submit to various forms of authority. Even football ceases to have meaning if the players are allowed to do whatever they want, whenever they want, to whomever they want. And that's what I believe the tribunal was trying to tell Mr. Dyer.

When the apostle Paul wrote Romans 13, admonishing Christians to be subject to those in authority, he didn't specify that the admonition was contingent upon the authority being to our liking or convenience. Rome certainly wasn't, from Paul's perspective. Yet he upheld law and order.

Similarly, David didn't show respect for Saul only so long as Saul was a good king, good friend, and good father-in-law. He considered him the "Lord's anointed," even when Saul's administration was at its lowest.

That kind of relationship to authority is a bit old-fashioned these days. But we might be better off if there were a little more of it around.

LIVING IN A MIXED-UP WORLD

In God We (Some, Anyway) Trust (Somewhat)

In several states legislation that allows or mandates the words "In God We Trust" to be posted in public buildings has been passed or is pending.

Many religious people see the move as a great victory for the cause of righteousness. But to the American Civil Liberties Union, it's the use of taxpayer money to fund unlawful, government-established religion.

Atheists and agnostics aren't likely supporters—since they've already decided they don't trust in God. And although the Christian majority in the United States pays lip service to such trust, our actions call our assertions into question. For example:

Television's faith healers promise that God can be depended on to intervene miraculously on behalf of the sincere soul. Doesn't the Bible say in Matthew 21:22: "If you believe, you will receive whatever you ask for in prayer" (NIV)? Yet these practitioners of faith still buy insurance for their multimillion-dollar production facilities—just in case.

We preachers urge our congregations to follow Jesus' words in the Sermon on the Mount: "Therefore I tell you, do not worry about your life, what you will eat or drink; or about you body, what you will wear. . . . But seek first [God's] kingdom and his righteousness, and all these things will be given to you as well" (Matthew 6:25-33, NIV). Then we go home to monitor our IRA, 401(k), and other retirement funds—lamenting that our church doesn't take seriously enough our need for a decent retirement nest egg.

Certain Christian ministries take as their motto: "Not by might nor by power, but by my Spirit" (Zechariah 4:6, NIV). But they still hire Madison Avenue types to formulate their image-building and fund-raising strategies.

In God We (Some, Anyway) Trust (Somewhat)

People of faith find solace in the psalmist David's assertion that "a thousand may fall at your side, ten thousand at your right hand, but it will not come near you" (Psalm 91:7, NIV). Yet we cast our ballots for the political candidates who promise to make our military—already the most lethal in the world—even bigger and stronger.

In Mark 9:14-32 is the story of a desperate man who asked Jesus to heal his demon-possessed son.

"Everything is possible for him who believes," Jesus said.

The man replied, "I do believe."

Then it suddenly struck him how hollow his assertion was. So he immediately added, "Help me overcome my unbelief!" (verses 23, 24, NIV).

It's a story worth considering before we glibly bandy about the phrase "In God We Trust."

If the constitutional issues raised by the government-funded display of these words don't give us pause, then perhaps a concern for truth in advertising will. After all, didn't God Himself say something about not bearing false witness?

And I trust that He meant what He said.

LIVING IN A MIXED-UP WORLD

Leveling the Acceptable

When I was living in Victoria, Australia, a few years ago, the state faced its highest road toll in 10 years (more than 800 deaths), and traffic authorities were clamping down in an attempt to reduce road deaths.

The concern was commendable. But it was also incongruous. If the road toll were the *lowest* in 10 years, attempts toward stricter road rules would have been unlikely—although several hundred people would still have been dying. In reality, the goal wasn't to *eliminate* road deaths, but simply to bring the number of deaths to an "acceptable level."

While we probably could never *totally* do away with road deaths, we could certainly bring the number down to a handful per year if we wanted to. The fact is, we don't really want to—and I'm talking about the average driver, not the traffic authorities. The adjustment would be too drastic for our time-pressured lifestyles.

We've decided that we'd rather sacrifice a few hundred people each year than have to drive 20 or 30 miles per hour on the open road and slower in built-up areas. Society's values concerning time and money mean we're prepared to work toward limiting the number of road deaths only so long as it doesn't *unduly* affect our ease of mobility.

We'll accept a speed reduction of five or 10 miles per hour—albeit grudgingly. Older drivers won't complain if the law places more restrictions on the young. And nondrinkers don't mind how many extra breath tests are given.

But we'd feel it unreasonable to be forced to drive in the conservative manner required to all but eradicate the road-death problem. That's asking too much. In other words, lives are important—but only to a point. We're happy to accept a calculated risk if the benefits are high enough.

But my point isn't really about driving habits and road deaths. It's about the "acceptable level" principle, to which most of us (perhaps unwittingly) subscribe in many areas of life.

In an article in *Rolling Stone* magazine a few years ago entitled "The Fighting Irish," writer P. J. O'Rourke quoted British home secretary Reginald Maulding as saying several years earlier that the violence in Northern Ireland had reached an "acceptable level."

O'Rourke found it difficult to conceive of an *"acceptable level of violence."* It's as if violence is being treated in much the same manner as "the air-quality index in an American city."

In fact, air pollution itself is but another example of how we're prepared to settle for an "acceptable level" (or even an unacceptable level) rather than make the lifestyle changes necessary to eradicate the problem.

And how many of us act as if we believe there's an acceptable level of immorality, an acceptable level of dishonesty, an acceptable level of selfishness, an acceptable level of pride, an acceptable level of materialism, or even an acceptable level of alcohol or recreational drug use?

How many of us feel secure because our jealousy, our failure to control our temper, our use of certain expletives when upset, our gossiping, our lack of concern for those in need are all at least within what we consider an acceptable level of character inadequacy?

How many of us feel that it would be unreasonable to expect the degree of perseverence and diligence required to make these areas of life what they really should be?

While God forgives our shortcomings, I can't imagine Him looking at our mixed-up world and saying that, even though the situation isn't ideal, it's at least at an "acceptable level."

LIVING IN A MIXED-UP WORLD

No High School Bible Classes, Please

Eighty-seven percent of callers in a recent newspaper phone poll favored teaching the Bible in public high schools. The argument goes like this: If high moral values existed when the Bible was prominent in the classroom decades ago, then reinstating the Bible will bring back better behavior.

No one would like to see moral revival more than I would. So let's suppose for a moment that Bible teaching is included in the curriculum.

First, who is qualified to teach? If a teacher has a string of degrees in comparative religion, ancient Middle Eastern literature, or ancient history but believes that the Bible is merely a collection of myths and questionable history, how much moral regeneration can we expect? As the teacher presents it, the Bible is essentially no better or worse than the writings of Jean-Paul Sartre or Aristotle or Charles Manson.

If I as a parent believe that the Bible is divinely inspired and that Jesus is the Savior of the world, I'm not likely to sit back contentedly while some academic agnostic minimizes the significance of something I believe in so strongly. And as a Christian, would I want my child's biblical instruction to come from a Hindu, Buddhist, or Muslim?

In fact, I would probably urge the school board to establish some litmus test of orthodoxy for Bible teachers. Forget the constitutional provisions for separation of church and state; the school board would have to hire or not hire on the basis of religious orthodoxy if it's going to please me as a parent.

If we're prepared to make religious orthodoxy a test for a Bible teacher in a government-funded school, then ultimately we may be tempted to try more of the same. Why shouldn't we make religious orthodoxy a test for the coach, the science teacher, the history teacher, or the English teacher? After all, aren't these people shaping the values of our children?

I'm a preacher. I earn my living by promoting the Bible. Every week in my sermon I uphold the Bible as the place to look for answers to life's really big questions. I believe the Bible tells how to ensure that we gain salvation, and it also provides guidelines on how to live in the here and now.

But there are major differences between my weekly sermon and a Bible class in a public high school. For starters, I make it clear right up front what I'm trying to do.

I don't say I'm looking at the Bible as simply history or literature. I'm totally frank about the fact that I view the Bible as the Word of God. I'm trying to strengthen the faith of Christians who already believe and make believers—more specifically, Christians—out of those who don't yet believe.

I want the Bible presented with conviction. I don't want my children exposed to some indifferent, anemic, ho-hum presentation of the Scriptures. The Bible is too special for that.

On the other hand, I don't want the children of my atheist, Muslim, or Hindu neighbors compelled to listen to a government-funded presentation of the intensity and conviction that I believe the Bible deserves.

I oppose teaching the Bible in public high school, not because I hold the Bible and my Christian faith in low regard. Rather, I oppose it because I hold them in such high regard.

LIVING IN A MIXED-UP WORLD

No Prayer, Please

A slight majority of respondents to a recent survey say they want a law calling for prayer in public schools.

I don't.

Yet it would seem I should. I'm a pastor. I get paid to pray for and with people. I encourage people to pray. I believe in prayer. So why would I ever oppose it?

Because such legislation would erode a critical freedom granted by the establishment clause of the First Amendment, which ensures that government won't create a state religion. Legislation for prayer in public schools may be well intended, but it's an inappropriate cure for society's moral problems.

Anyone who has ever tried to offer a prayer acceptable to Catholics, Protestants, Jews, Muslims, Buddhists, and Hindus knows how impossible it is. The state could never write prayers that would satisfy everyone. Inevitably they would please some (the majority religions, probably) and offend others (the minority religions). And even a period of silence to facilitate prayer is a subtle but dangerous step.

I believe that most Christians view prayer as something they can do silently, wherever and whenever they choose, for as long as they choose, without altering body posture and without specific equipment. So a period of silence would allow most Christians to pray.

However, suppose a student subscribes to a belief system in which prayer must be audible. Suppose it would be a sacrilege not to bow to the ground, facing a specific direction, at specific times of the day.

Suppose prayer in this system must continue for a long period. Suppose prayer can't be offered under a roof but must be outdoors.

Suppose prayer requires a prayer shawl, a prayer mat, or equipment that would disrupt those students who are simply bowing their heads.

The government would need to accommodate a multitude of prayer options or be guilty of religious favoritism. If the government refuses to make such accommodations, it in essence is stating that non-Christians aren't worthy of special provisions to make prayer possible, but Christians are.

And what about atheists and agnostics? Are they going to have to bow their heads in a show of respect they don't feel or else risk being looked down on?

Don't misunderstand me. I'm biased in favor of Christianity, and I wish everyone would pray. But I don't want the government's help. I don't want legislation that, however unintended, might favor Baptists over Unitarians, Protestants over Catholics, or Christians over Buddhists.

Understandably, the government wants good, law-abiding citizens. But whether that goal is best achieved by praying in the name of Jesus, by praying to Allah, or by rejecting religion altogether shouldn't concern the state.

And when it becomes the state's concern, the First Amendment's establishment clause is well on its way toward being abolished.

LIVING IN A MIXED-UP WORLD

Protecting One's Investment

During the past few years a number of studies have shown that the average father in the United States spends almost no time with his children.

The problem isn't limited to the United States, nor is the breakdown merely between father and children. Changing values, financial pressures, and an increased emphasis on professional achievement have taken their toll on family relations. The long-term implications are frightening.

The absence of clearly defined role models is producing bewildered children. Failure to express affection adequately is creating a generation less capable of affection. And the pace of life leaves husbands and wives simply drifting apart.

But what, you might say, does all this have to do with the title—"Protecting One's Investment"? Simply this: If a father's sense of paternal responsibility and moral obligation isn't a sufficient incentive for him to spend more and higher-quality time with his family, then perhaps noting certain financial realities will provide the needed motivation. For, after all, "where your treasure is, there will your heart be also" (Matthew 6:21).

A family constitutes the greatest single investment that many men are likely to ever make. Simple business sense dictates that we should seek the highest return possible.

Obviously, I'm not saying that we should love our families simply because we've invested money in them. However, I do think it helpful to recognize that were we to make a similar investment in almost any other area, we wouldn't treat it with the indifference with which we sometimes treat our own flesh and blood.

Families are perishable commodities. Not only do they fall apart if they're not cared for properly, but they also come with a built-in hourglass. When the sand has run out, no more return will be paid on the investment, at least not in this world. Therefore, now is the time to be gaining the benefits, to be collecting the dividends. And herein lies the beauty of this investment.

In the financial world people making capital-growth investments must avoid collecting income or dividends along the way, or they jeopardize their long-term returns. In the family, the reverse is true: the more dividends collected daily, the greater the chances for long-term returns.

Where else, I ask, can you find an investment like that?

Agreeing With God

In his book *What Return Can I Make?* psychiatrist M. Scott Peck tells the story of a little girl in the Philippines who claimed that Jesus regularly came and talked to her.

Soon word of this extraordinary phenomenon spread beyond the village where she lived.

A high-ranking church leader became intrigued. Was this a miraculous case of divinity communing with humanity? Was it a hoax? Was it just the vivid imaginings of a child?

The church leader arranged an interview in which the little girl described how Jesus talked with her. What she said was convincing. But the leader wanted more objective evidence.

"The next time Jesus talks with you," he said, "I want you to do me a favor. Ask Jesus what sins I confessed to Him during the past week."

She promised she would. And they arranged to meet again.

At their next appointment the church leader asked if Jesus had talked to her since they last met.

"Yes," she said, "He has."

"And did you remember to ask what sins I had confessed?" he asked.

"I did."

"And what did Jesus say?"

"Jesus said He has forgotten the sins you confessed," the little girl answered without hesitation.

At this point Peck leaves the story (much to my consternation, because I wanted to hear the end of it!) and draws his lesson: Whether the little girl was a shrewd con artist or a modern-day mouthpiece for God, she spoke a vital spiritual truth.

The fact is that when God forgives, He forgives totally. And He doesn't keep trotting out our sins. Nor does He want us to. In 1 John 1:9 we read: "If we confess our sins, he is faithful and just to forgive us our sins."

The Greek word translated "confess" is made up of two parts—*homo,* meaning "the same," and *logeo,* meaning "to say." When we confess, we're really just saying the same thing that God has already said. And what is that?

"For all have sinned, and come short of the glory of God" (Romans 3:23). "All we like sheep have gone astray" (Isaiah 53:6). "If we say that we have no sin, we deceive ourselves" (1 John 1:8).

Confession is agreeing with God.

God has stated that we're *all* sinners. In confession we say, in effect, "You're absolutely right, Lord; I *am* a sinner. And just in case there was any question, look at what I've just done to prove it. Now, please forgive me and cleanse me from my unrighteousness."

But it's not enough to agree with God that we're sinners. We must also agree that He can and will forgive. We must accept the fact that we *are* forgiven. And then we must cease bringing up the matter again and again.

Our job is to confess our sins. God's job is to dispose of them. And He does it thoroughly. Micah 7:19 promises that He'll cast our "sins into the depths of the sea"—totally out of sight.

If our sins are no longer in God's sight, why should they be in ours? If He forgets them—as the little girl in the story so rightly pointed out—why can't we forget them and get on with living the life He designed us for?

The problem is that too many of us don't really believe that God forgives—at least not readily. Unlike Abraham, we aren't fully persuaded that what God has promised He is able also to perform (Romans 4:21). We treat confession almost as a form of penance and try to convince God of our remorse by repeatedly acknowledging our wrongdoing. We seem to feel that confidence in God's ability to forgive means that we're taking sin lightly.

The reality is that grace comes into its own where it's most desperately needed. And if we're to err in focusing too much on *God's* grace or too much on *our* failure, let it be on the side of God's grace.

Only when we experience God's forgiveness can we have the experience *The Living Bible* describes in Romans 5:1, 2: "Since we have been made right in God's sight by faith in his promises," "we confidently and joyfully look forward to actually becoming all that God has had in mind for us to be."

The God of the universe can forgive and forget human failings. The question is, can we?

GOD'S WORD AND OUR UNDERSTANDINGS

Balancing the Equation

What I'm about to say is not new. It's something that Christians have discussed and debated at least since the time of the apostles. But sometimes we need to be reminded of things we already know. And I refer here to the respective roles of grace, faith, and behavior.

Grace, I would suggest, is that aspect of God's character that allows Him to love and accept us even when we're unlovely and—at least from our perspective—totally unacceptable. Yet He loves and accepts us nonetheless.

Viewed from another perspective, grace is also *our experience* of this characteristic of God. It occurs when we accept His acceptance. It is the light breaking through. It is the realization that God *does* accept us, even though we're sinners, if we'll but accept His acceptance.

Theologian Paul Tillich has described this experience as being "struck by grace." C. S. Lewis speaks of being "surprised by joy." And this experience is made possible by faith.

There are many good definitions of faith (see Hebrews 11:1), and no doubt all of them have their strengths and weaknesses. However, for me the best practical definition is that *faith is action.*

Probably most of us have heard the story of the man who was preparing to push a wheelbarrow across Niagara Falls on a tightrope. Turning to the crowd, he asked who thought he could do it. When most of the onlookers shouted their confidence in his ability, he pointed to a man near the front and said, "Then get into the wheelbarrow."

Real faith, it seems to me, is believing so much that something is truth that we act upon it. If we cannot demonstrate our faith in action, then our faith is suspect.

But even though faith can accomplish some wonderful things, it merely appropriates—lays hold of—something that's already there. In the case of salvation, if God didn't love and accept sinful humans, all the faith in the world would accomplish nothing.

And just in case we develop an inflated opinion of the value of our faith, the apostle Paul points out that even faith isn't something we create ourselves. God gives it to us. "For it is by grace you have been saved, through faith—and this not from yourselves, it is the gift of God—not by works, so that no one can boast" (Ephesians 2:8, NIV).

Where does behavior fit into all this? Simply like this. God wants the best for His creatures. He designed us, and He wants us to live according to the purposes for which we were designed. He doesn't want us to settle for a subhuman existence.

So the Bible places great emphasis on behavior—not as a way of earning God's favor, but because it is important to live the way God designed for us to live.

We don't pat ourselves on the back for not having robbed any banks today, or for not having killed anyone today, because that's simply expected behavior. In the same way, we shouldn't pat ourselves on the back for having quit swearing, or for paying tithe, or for helping those in need—because that too is simply what's expected of someone whom God has created.

If our emphasis on grace and faith makes us soft-pedal the need for proper behavior, then we aren't presenting biblical truth. The gospels are saturated with the truth of God's acceptance of sinners. But they also contain the Sermon on the Mount. The apostle Paul makes it clear that no one can earn his or her way to heaven—but he also wrote Romans 12 and Galatians 6.

Conversely, if our emphasis on behavior makes us think that we can earn our way to heaven, or that we can impress God with our inherent goodness, then we're deluding ourselves.

As with all things in the Christian experience, balance is the key. Some people spend a lot of time analyzing how the spiritual equation should be balanced. And they have their complicated theories even on how the balance should be described. But unless the balance is reflected in our lives, the theory is empty and of little use.

GOD'S WORD AND OUR UNDERSTANDINGS

Concerning Camels

When Christ said, "It is easier for a camel to go through the eye of a needle, than for a rich man to enter into the kingdom of God" (Mark 10:25), He provided fuel for a debate that has lasted nearly 2,000 years.

Some have suggested that if the word "camel" were altered slightly in the original language, it could be read "rope." Thus Jesus was speaking mild hyperbole rather than total absurdity. A more common suggestion is that Jesus was referring to a small gate in the wall of Jerusalem, purportedly called The Eye of a Needle, through which a camel could pass only if it were unloaded and made to get down on its knees.

The Wycliffe Bible Commentary points out, however: "The idea that *the eye of a needle,* referred to here, was a small gate through which a camel could enter only on his knees is without warrant. The word for *needle* refers specifically to a sewing needle. Furthermore, Jesus was not talking about what man considers possible, but about what seems to be impossible (cf. verse 27). With man it is impossible for *a camel to go through the eye* of a sewing needle."

While destroying such alternative interpretations leaves the rich feeling vulnerable, the poor are in danger of becoming smug: To them, Jesus obviously is talking about people who earn large incomes, have swimming pools, drive expensive cars, and take exotic vacations on their yachts or at their vacation cabins. Or is He?

Just whom do we mean when we talk about the "rich"? Is it the conspicuous consumers we have just described? Is it those who have considerable net worth, even though they may live frugally? Or is it those whose incomes are in the top 25, 15, or 10 percent?

If we look at worldwide statistics, we discover that even those in the

United States who receive public assistance probably rank in the top 25 percent, and the majority of us would be in the top 15 percent.

Looked at from a global perspective, even the poor in North America, Western Europe, and several other areas are rich. So perhaps we should tread more gingerly in any attack upon rich people. Riches are relative, after all.

The key to understanding Jesus' comment is Mark 10:24. "Children, how hard it is for them that *trust in riches* to enter into the kingdom of God!" Christ's words are parallel to Paul's: "The *love of money* is the root of all evil" (1 Timothy 6:10).

Christ's concern isn't that people shouldn't be rich. Numerous heroes of the Bible were rich—Job, Abraham, Solomon, Nicodemus, Joseph of Arimathea. These people weren't condemned for their great wealth. Christ's concern is with materialism, not with *material*—and material*ism* can occur at any financial level.

If a man owns one goat and more than anything else wants to obtain a second goat, and if he sacrifices the things of eternal value in his struggle to acquire the additional goat, then he's a materialist—although he may have precious little material.

Be it the acquisition of a goat, a second room on a mud house, or a more attractive pair of sandals, if pursuit of such items causes a person to neglect obligations to God, family, or fellow humans, then that person stands condemned by God.

Quantity isn't significant. Attitude is. One person may be able to drive a luxury car while keeping his or her values in perspective. For another, the acquisition and maintenance of an old bicycle may be all-consuming.

Certainly there must come a point at which expenditure and consumption no longer can be justified. Humans have been placed on earth as God's stewards. We're to be channels through whom His blessings can be distributed to those in need. But we shouldn't be worrying about the absolute limits so much as the attitude.

In the truest sense, nothing we possess is our own. It's all God's. So there must be limits to how much we lavish life's bounties on ourselves in relation to the needs of the world around us. And when we look at the amount that our parents and grandparents needed to live, then compare it with what we probably consider essential, we may find ourselves in need of some sincere soul-searching.

Although undue concern for money is Christ's major concern, the danger is ever present that people who have riches may become attached to their riches—and such a danger exists for all who live in a world of affluence, even though we never may have thought of ourselves as rich. Riches aren't the problem; attachment is. Unfortunately, however, a strong connection often exists between the two.

More than a century ago Henry David Thoreau commented: "Most of the luxuries and many of the so-called comforts of life are not only not indispensable, but positive hindrances to the elevation of mankind." He likewise maintained that "a man is rich in proportion to the number of things he can afford to leave alone," and "the man is richest whose pleasures are the cheapest."

As for Christ's words in Mark 10, they mean what they say—and they have significance for all of us.

Consequences

When I was young I found great difficulty in understanding why God would "curse" the earth (Genesis 3:16-18) after Adam and Eve's sin. It almost seemed that sin in and of itself wasn't bad enough, so God rubbed a little salt into the wound.

I was even more concerned with the idea of the sins of the fathers being visited "upon the children unto the third and fourth generation" (Exodus 20:5). I knew enough about my family tree to feel it might just be time to settle the score. But that didn't seem fair. Why should God chastise me for something my great-grandfather did?

Similarly, I never took great comfort in the idea of God sending people delusions so that they would believe a lie and be damned (2 Thessalonians 2:11, 12). It didn't make sense. After all, with the powers that God has at His disposal, what chance did mere mortals have if He decided to delude them? And why would He want them to be damned?

From a relatively early age I've wrestled with the problem of the wages of sin. Does sin merely cause God to act differently toward the sinner, meting out punishments He feels are appropriate? Does sin bring its own reward, in a cause-and-effect manner? Or does sin bring some natural results *and* cause God to add some punishments of His own?

To put it another way: Are we punished *for* our sins, or are we punished *by* our sins? Or both? The answer we give has implications for how we'll view God. And is "punish" even the correct word to describe what comes in sin's wake?

Robert Ingersoll also wrestled with this issue. And his comment may be helpful. He said, "In nature there are neither rewards nor punishments; there are consequences."

Ingersoll wasn't the only person to recognize a certain incongruity in depicting God as inflicting the penalty (again, perhaps not the right word) for our transgressions.

Ellen White wrote: "We are not to regard God as waiting to punish the sinner for his sin. The sinner brings the punishment upon himself. His own actions start a train of circumstances that bring the sure result. Every act of transgression reacts upon the sinner, works in him a change of character, and makes it more easy for him to transgress again. By choosing to sin, men separate themselves from God, cut themselves off from the channel of blessing, and the sure result is ruin and death" (*The Seventh-day Adventist Bible Commentary,* Ellen G. White Comments, vol. 6, p. 1110).

Speaking about the ultimate destruction of the wicked, Ellen White says: "This is not an act of arbitrary power on the part of God. The rejecters of His mercy reap that which they have sown. God is the fountain of life; and when one chooses the service of sin, he separates from God, and thus cuts himself off from life. . . . By a life of rebellion, Satan and all who unite with him place themselves so out of harmony with God that His very presence is to them a consuming fire. The glory of Him who is love will destroy them" (*The Desire of Ages,* p. 764).

In an equally interesting passage, she says, "Every seed sown produces a harvest of its kind. So it is in human life. . . . God destroys no man. Everyone who is destroyed will have destroyed himself" (*Christ's Object Lessons,* pp. 84, 85).

In the modern world, when we speak of law we're usually referring to one of two kinds of law: judicial law or natural law. Judicial law seeks to govern by imposing punishments for unacceptable behavior.

Natural law, on the other hand, is merely a statement of fact about what is. It's a description. It contains no sense that something *must* behave in a certain way or be punished. It merely says that, granted certain conditions, something *will* behave in a certain way.

Natural law, as we know it, was unknown during the time of the Bible writers. Thus, all behavioral expectations—and the results for failure to live according to those expectations—are presented in terms of judicial law.

But is it possible that if the Bible writers were living today, they'd spend much more time talking about cause and effect? Could it be that they would, as Ellen White has done in some cases, speak more of consequences than of punishments?

And could it be that God isn't at all interested in rubbing salt into our wounds?

GOD'S WORD AND OUR UNDERSTANDINGS

Consistency, Please

Many who oppose ordaining women to pastoral ministry (or even as elders) point out, correctly, that the Bible contains no directive or precedent for it.

Many also argue that Paul's statements in 1 Corinthians 14:34, 35 and 1 Timothy 2:11-15 aren't based on culture, but describe a God-sanctioned order. However, before we unduly emphasize these arguments, we need to look at their implications. After all, consistency and credibility go hand in hand.

1. Understandably, the Bible provides no directive or precedent for many practices common in the church today—including the ordination of men to pastoral ministry.

The Bible says that the 12 apostles were ordained (Mark 3:14; Acts 1:22). It says that elders were ordained (Acts 14:23; Titus 1:5). It says that the apostles laid hands on the seven deacons (Acts 6:6). And hands were laid on Paul and Barnabas before their missionary journey (Acts 13:3). Futhermore, Paul declares that he was "ordained" (the word "ordained" can mean merely "appointed"—see various modern translations) "a preacher, and an apostle." He goes on to define his role more specifically as a "teacher of the Gentiles" (1 Timothy 2:7).

There's simply no New Testament reference to the ordination of pastors. And equating elders and pastors doesn't provide a solution. It merely creates a new problem of at least equal magnitude in a different arena. So, on the basis of Biblical precedent and directive, there's no more reason for pastors to be ordained than for teachers, Bible workers, or several other groups.

2. The fact that the Seventh-day Adventist Church has traditionally

not ordained its "deaconesses" (although it's happening occasionally now) raises interesting questions—because here's a case in which we *do* have biblical precedent. There was at least one female deacon in New Testament times (Romans 16:1, RSV; *The Seventh-day Adventist Bible Commentary,* vol. 6, p. 649)—despite the fact that the criteria for being a deacon, as for being an elder, included being the *husband* of one *wife* (1 Timothy 3:12)!

Granted, we don't know much about Phebe or about how women may have been selected and inaugurated as deacons, but we do have biblical precedent for women to serve in this capacity. Further, as a church we have recognized the *need* for women to play such a role. Thus we have established the office of "deaconess." So why have we traditionally not ordained women filling this role?

Has our withholding of ordination implied that we view the female *deacon's* (the word "deaconess" doesn't come from the Bible) role as different from, inferior to, or of lesser spiritual significance than that of the male deacon's role? But on what basis? Or does it reflect something about our culture's attitudes toward women and the role we'll allow them to play in things spiritual?

On the other hand, since we seem to have been quite comfortable accepting female deacons (as long as we call them "deaconesses" and don't ordain them—even though they really perform the same function as deacons), would we also accept female pastors and female elders as long as we called them "pastoresses" and "elderesses" and didn't ordain them—even though they perform the same function as the male pastor or male elder?

3. If the crystal-clear statements of 1 Corinthians 14:34, 35 and 1 Timothy 2:11-15 aren't based on culture and local considerations but describe a God-sanctioned order, then why have we allowed women to speak in our churches—particularly in our Sabbath schools—throughout the history of our denomination?

How can we justify trotting out Paul's statements only when women's *ordination* is mentioned? The statements either are or aren't influenced by culture. If they aren't, then women should immediately be banned from speaking in churches. We can't have it both ways.

There may be valid theological or sociological arguments against ordaining women. But if we deny them ordination on the basis of the arguments I've just analyzed, then we'd better prepare for major changes in church practice.

Or we'd better prepare to live with some credibility-destroying inconsistencies.

Does Suicide Preclude Salvation?

Every year millions of people go through the heart-rending experience of saying an earthly goodbye to a son or daughter, husband or wife, mother or father. Terrible though such a parting is, the anguish is multiplied many times over when the death is self-inflicted.

Beyond the natural grief lies the social stigma. Beyond the social stigma is the guilt—"If only I had . . . it might have . . ."—irrespective of how undeserved such self-condemnation may be. Perhaps more devastating still, at least for the Christian, is the question Has my loved one forfeited salvation? In answer to that question, an examination of real-life experiences in Bible times might offer insight.

Having squandered the productive years of his life in debauched living, Samson found himself virtually a beast of burden in a Philistine prison. He certainly hadn't fulfilled God's plan for his life. To the contrary, for the most part his life had brought dishonor to God.

Suddenly Samson was in a situation in which his life's ambition seemed, to a great degree, within his grasp. But for that goal to be realized he must—at least as he saw it from his limited perspective—sacrifice his own life. Samson chose to die. And, his manner of death notwithstanding, his name appears on the honor roll of faith in Hebrews 11.

Years earlier a young Canaanite woman whose morals left much to be desired found herself in a situation in which she felt, based on her limited perspective, that she must either bear false witness or condemn two houseguests to death—to say nothing of herself and her entire family.

According to Rahab's rather simplistic ethical code, the course to be pursued was clear-cut: she lied. Not only was her and her family's life spared, but she likewise receives mention in the honor roll of faith.

Furthermore, there's at least circumstantial evidence that the Messiah was born in her lineage.

Israel's most popular king, also an ancestor of Christ, was an impetuous but lovable man. Although God had outlined sanctuary ritual down to the minutiae, and although certain activities were reserved exclusively for the priesthood, David nonetheless helped himself to the shewbread when he and his men were hungry. As he viewed it from his finite perspective, that was the only food available.

Not only was David called "a man after mine [God's] own heart" and mentioned in the honor roll of faith, but Christ Himself implicitly condoned what he did (Matthew 12:3).

The common denominator of the preceding examples is that each individual—because of extenuating circumstances—violated an express command of God's. Yet in each case the offender was fully accepted by God.

It would be reckless and irresponsible to extrapolate from these isolated instances a position that humans can break the laws of God with impunity. On the other hand, they serve as reminders that man's ways are not God's ways and that man's thoughts are not God's thoughts. They should likewise remind us that, while humans look only on the outward appearance, God can read the heart.

But where does this leave us with regard to suicide and salvation?

Should anyone use these examples simply as a license to do what God has prohibited, they may be playing Russian roulette with their salvation—and the odds may not be the relatively favorable five to one. In contrast, however, we must recognize that we don't know the pain, the pressure, or the anguish with which another person is wrestling—even if we ourselves have been through apparently similar circumstances. We view the situation only externally and can't discern motives.

In the situation in which a person has committed suicide, the examples cited provide a strong biblical basis for hope. God is the judge; we aren't. We can take great consolation in the mercy that He granted to other human beings whose offense wasn't altogether different from that of our friend or relative.

After all, would He love our friend or relative any less?

God on Trial

At some stage we all complain about not getting a fair deal in life. Our boss is unreasonable. Our children are ungrateful. Our spouse is unfeeling. The government charges too much tax and provides too few services. And the list goes on.

I've even heard some people complain that God is unjust. That He should do more than He's doing for some, and less than He's doing for others. That He's too demanding. That He doesn't realize how complex and difficult our world is. How can He expect so much of us?

Most of us are so caught up in worrying about our own predicament that we never even think about the predicament that God is in. You see, in a sense, He's on trial. And you and I are the jurors. What will be our decision? Just what kind of justice will we mete out?

The biblical account of Adam and Eve (Genesis 3) is all about God's character being placed on trial. In this story God doesn't act like some bad-tempered king. He doesn't come to Adam and Eve and say, "Look, you're not good enough for Me. I don't want you to be My subjects anymore." Rather, Adam and Eve, by their choices and their actions, tell God that He isn't worthy to be their Master.

The serpent tells them that if they eat of the forbidden fruit, their eyes will be opened and they'll be like gods, knowing good and evil. That sounds exciting.

Be like God! Not be mere humans! Be like God Himself!

Of course, their choice has profound implications. In essence they're saying that God is unjust. That He's keeping back all the good from them. That His way of doing things isn't the most fulfilling. In short, they judge God and find Him to be a tyrant.

Today you and I have to make the same kind of decision about God. It may be conscious or unconscious. If we judge Him to be kind, loving, and good, we'll try to live the way He has outlined for us. If He's a tyrant, a killjoy, an old fuddy-duddy, then we'll ignore Him and do as we please. He won't be worth listening to.

In the final analysis the way we live demonstrates how we've judged God. And a quick look around our world suggests that the jury of humanity doesn't place much credence in God's testimony about Himself.

The worst thing about misjudging God is that it leads us to misunderstand ourselves. God created us in His image. And more than that, we grow into the image of the God—or god—we worship. If we misjudge God, we break our relationship with Him. And that has extremely negative results for us.

The Bible is the human "operator's manual," as it were, published by our Maker. But if we judge Him to be incompetent, we naturally disregard the instructions He gives. And that leads to pain, sorrow, and even death.

Often it may not be so much a conscious decision on our part. Maybe it's an unconscious belief that we know better than He does. That life will be better if we do things our own way.

God can't really state His case any clearer. Jesus came to earth to demonstrate what God is really like. But even He was misunderstood and put to death.

Justice is difficult to find. And until justice is worked out on a cosmic scale, it won't be properly dealt with on the human scale.

Sure, the world's unjust. And it's painful when injustice hits us personally. However, there's some comfort in the fact that God knows how it feels.

GOD'S WORD AND OUR UNDERSTANDINGS

Of Creeds and Concrete

Some time ago I heard a speaker say that "if a denominational worker doesn't believe *every one* of the Adventist Church's 27 fundamental beliefs, that person is being dishonest in accepting his or her paycheck."

At first blush the statement seems the epitome of orthodoxy. After all, if the 27 fundamental beliefs are the agreed-upon beliefs of Seventh-day Adventists, church employees certainly should be stalwart supporters. And the same principle applies to all who take the name Seventh-day Adventist. However, the foregoing statement actually runs counter to our statement of beliefs—unless it's carefully qualified!

The preamble to the 27 fundamental beliefs states: "Seventh-day Adventists accept the Bible as their only creed and hold certain fundamental beliefs to be the teaching of the Holy Scriptures. These beliefs, as set forth here, constitute the church's understanding and expression of the teaching of Scripture. Revision of these statements may be expected at a General Conference session when the church is led by the Holy Spirit to a fuller understanding of Bible truth or finds better language in which to express the teachings of God's Holy Word."

The preamble may well be the most important component of our statement of belief—because it lays down the ground rules. And if I understand it correctly, as Adventists we believe it highly significant that we haven't followed many other Christian bodies in writing a creed.

Because we believe in progressive revelation, and because we recognize human frailty, we don't want the current description of our commonly held beliefs to be set in concrete. We want to allow for clearer understanding, for clearer expression. Thus, we have opted for a "statement of belief" instead of a "creed."

This concern to safeguard the potential for change is crucial. But we must be careful on at least three fronts.

First, we must guard against becoming holier-than-other-Christians by reading more than is warranted into the distinction between a "creed" and a "statement of belief." My dictionary defines *creed* as "any formula of religious belief."

Those Christian groups with long-established creeds could just as easily be said to have a "statement of belief" (however set in concrete it may be). And Adventists could accurately be described as having a "creed"—it's just one that's subject to revision. In short, the terms don't indicate as much as we've often assumed. What really counts is the practice.

Second, we must guard against letting our statement of belief turn into a creed that's set in concrete. And statements such as the one from the speaker I quoted at the beginning help make that very thing happen. That statement inadvertently precludes the possibility of change. Let me illustrate.

If our statement of belief were ever to be changed, the thinking of a majority of the voting participants at a General Conference session would have had to change first. And it would probably have been a slow change over a period of years. Does this mean that those who felt convicted that the statement needed changing were dishonest in accepting their paychecks or in calling themselves Adventists before the change took place?

And what about those who disagree with a change that has just been approved by the majority at a GC session—those who prefer the statement the way it was? Do they arrive at the session as loyal members, yet leave disloyal?

Third, having emphasized that we must be open to change (which implies tolerance and room for a degree of individuality), we must be careful that we not use our personal freedom as license to promulgate every belief we might happen to hold.

Some of our church's greatest pioneers had idiosyncracies when it came to belief. But most also had an overriding loyalty that sought the good of the body rather than the right to ride a hobbyhorse. Thus, I would suggest that *loyalty* is a far more crucial consideration than full agreement with the choice of every word in our statement of beliefs.

As with all aspects of religion, balance is the key. Too much emphasis on the need for agreement with our statement of belief can, by default, create a creed. And too light a view of the statement's importance creates anarchy. But a balanced view creates an atmosphere of both fellowship and ongoing discovery.

RELATING TO CHRIST'S BRIDE

By Their Loot Ye Shall Know Them

Several years ago I sat next to a Muslim while flying from Melbourne to Perth. He told me that he had originally come from India. Now in the clothing design business in Australia, he was traveling to check on some of his retail outlets.

When I told him I was a minister of religion and an editor, he immediately questioned me about what I thought of the scandals surrounding several American televangelists at that time. Then he followed up with a question that set me back: "Do you believe in God?" Now, I've been asked that question before, but never after I've just told my questioner that I'm a minister of religion.

As our conversation continued, it became clear that this Muslim had come to think that many—if not all—Christian leaders, institutions, and activities were exclusively concerned with getting money. He'd long had reservations about certain practices condoned by Christians, and from his perspective, God seemed incidental in most Christian activity.

Fortunately, there was at least one exception—Mother Teresa, whose charitable work he'd seen while visiting Calcutta. Mother Teresa was Christianity's one and only redeeming feature for him.

As I pondered his comments, I thought of the disciple Peter's description of religious practitioners who are in it for their own material gain: "Many will follow their shameful ways and will bring the way of truth into disrepute," he wrote. "In their greed these teachers will exploit you with stories they have made up" (2 Peter 2:2, 3, NIV).

Jesus taught that those who are leaders are in fact the servants of others—not lords over them. The higher the leadership position, the higher the level of accountability to those being served.

"The kings of the Gentiles lord it over them," Jesus said. "But you are not to be like that. Instead, the greatest among you should be like the youngest, and the one who rules like the one who serves. For who is greater, the one who is at the table or the one who serves? Is it not the one who is at the table? But I am among you as one who serves" (Luke 22:25-27, NIV).

Not only are people justified in expecting simplicity and accountability on the part of religious leaders; they should also be able to expect the same of all people who occupy positions of significance.

The president of a giant corporation shouldn't be begrudged his large salary. But it's reasonable for those under him to expect him not to abuse the system to feather his nest even more.

Politicians may be able to live at a high standard because of their wealth or because of judicious use of their salaries. But voters are justified in expecting them not to take advantage of the system just because they're insiders and know how to manipulate things for their own benefit.

Ideally, parents occupy a place of authority and respect in the eyes of their children. Nevertheless, they mustn't forget that their status places them under obligation to their children.

The fact that many of today's famous media preachers live like lords is questionable from a biblical perspective. But their obligations certainly aren't limited to fiscal responsibility. Even worse is the fact that too often their moral behavior is less than exemplary—despite the fact that they seek to project the image of being the last bastions of defense against immorality. Ironically, the standard set by these preachers' own words is the criterion by which the public judges their lives.

So how should we respond to the moral shortfalls of spiritual leaders?

We could cease to support religious endeavors altogether. We could write off religion as a mere racket, controlled by people in it to get what they can. Or we can remember that there still are Mother Teresas, who aren't in it for what they can get. And we can also remember our own failures, and that it's only the person without sin who can cast the first stone.

RELATING TO CHRIST'S BRIDE

Dropping the Cultured Stones

As a youth growing up in the Midwest, I believed that only in the Midwest did people speak English the way it was meant to be spoken. That's why God spoke English with a Midwestern accent!

Then the vision splendid faded. I spent a year "south of the border," where Americans were seen as gringos, not as God's favored people. As I ate Mexican, slept Mexican, and lived Mexican—while watching the parade of moneyed American tourists pass through—I began to understand why many Mexicans felt as they did about Americans.

Later I studied the American Revolution from the perspective of a history lecturer at Newbold College in England. To my chagrin, I was forced to acknowledge that there might be more than one way to view the Anglo-American altercation of 1776-1783.

After spending some 10 years experiencing the vast distances between points in Australia, I *almost* came to understand how seemingly rational, well-balanced people can turn into masochistic maniacs once they get behind the steering wheel of a car!

The most valuable experiences of my life have come from living, working, and studying in a number of cultures. And I've discovered, painfully, that culture has played a much greater role than I realized in what I've considered acceptable or unacceptable in the area of practical Christianity.

Most of us tolerate, to at least a limited degree, the varied outlooks of different cultures. But we have much greater difficulty showing tolerance for subcultures *within* our own culture. Sometimes we forget that there *are* distinct subcultures. And over the past few decades they've become quite clearly defined.

For example, the mind-set of the average young person (under age 30, say) differs radically in many ways from that of the average 70-year-old. Indeed, the two groups are effectively living in totally different cultures.

Because both speak English with the same accent, they themselves often don't see the great cultural gulf. But they experience it. And they don't show the same tolerance they might show toward someone of a visibly different culture.

At the turn of the century it was crucial to give respect to people in certain positions. When I was a student we were still carefully instructed in such niceties as who should be introduced first when introducing two people. We had to treat with deference the person with the "higher" station in life.

Today's young person couldn't be bothered with such seemingly senseless regulations. After all, as long as each person knows the identity of the other, who cares?

As far as young people are concerned, forget the titles. They prefer to relate to a person as an individual rather than as someone who has achieved a certain rank. They prefer first names. They prefer to equalize rather than differentiate.

When I was growing up, every young man had a suit—or at least a sport jacket and dress trousers—to wear to such formal gatherings as Sabbath school and the church service. But to a great degree such attire has gone by the board in the culture of the young.

I recently visited a youth Sabbath school and noted that of the 32 males present, 24 were wearing sweaters. Only eight wore suits or sport jackets.

Of those eight, four weren't wearing a tie, or were wearing a brightly colored shirt, or had the sleeves of their jacket pulled up in a way that certainly wouldn't have been acceptable when I was growing up. The scene would have been totally different in the senior Sabbath school of that same church.

In today's youth culture, comfort has become a major criterion. Young people won't put up with discomfort merely to please an older generation who have put up with discomfort all their lives. Such things as ties and traditional suits are an optional extra for many young people. Many prefer what older people consider casual styles—though they aren't necessarily casual in the minds of the young.

But the cultural differences between young and old aren't limited to introductions and clothing. The list goes on—and on. For example, most young people like music that speaks to them in a language and style to which they can immediately relate.

Without question, the lyrics of some of the religious music young people like are whimsical and trite. But we shouldn't be surprised.

About the time the Seventh-day Adventist Church was being formed, a wave of whimsical and trite religious music swept across North America. But it spoke to the American people in the context of their times and culture, and in a language to which they could relate.

Despite shouts of "Unacceptable!" from many quarters back then, some of that type of music has made it into today's hymnals and has great meaning for many of us.

But if we're honest, some of the hymns we sing have words that make the lyrics to some of the young people's music sound positively Shakespearean.

Now, I'm not knocking traditional music. Nor am I suggesting that all music should be accepted willy-nilly. However, music has to speak within a cultural context if it's going to reach the heart. And what speaks to your culture won't necessarily speak to your parents' or your children's.

Because of the complexities of different cultural tastes, we've never been in such great need of tolerance. We've never so badly needed a concerted effort to understand what makes others think and act as they do.

We've never before faced a situation in which society was changing so rapidly. We've never seen such a pronounced development of cultures within cultures. We've never been at such a loss to know how to relate to what's going on.

In light of this, young people need to try to understand just how important certain forms of behavior are to older people. They need to try to understand the value system that calls for such behavior. They need to try to figure out what makes older people tick.

Older people aren't just a group of fuddy-duddies who are totally out of touch. Partly, maybe. But not totally! They have years of experience. Inevitably this closes their minds to some things—but it opens them to others.

Young people would benefit from sincerely attempting to understand the thinking and concerns of the older generation. Before too many years pass, today's young people will look at tomorrow's young people and wonder how they could possibly think and behave as they do.

They'll wonder why the youth have rejected their values. They'll shake their heads at what seems to be a culture run amok.

On the other hand, nothing broadens the minds of older people as much as an attempt to understand the mind-set of the young. And if they can't understand it, they should be less hasty to criticize it.

Why do young people seem to have an aversion to the formalities of yesteryear? Is there something to be said for their efforts toward a more one-class society? Does their emphasis on intimacy destroy respect? Or do they simply show their respect in different ways? What has been gained and what has been lost?

In the church, the older generation to a great degree still holds the power. And as long as they hold that power, they have a duty to try to determine how much of young people's behavior is purely a matter of culture and taste, and how much it involves immutable spiritual values.

There may be times when those with years on their side will have to pull the youth into line. They may have to demand conformity in certain areas—"or else." But they must do it cautiously, as little as possible, humbly and only after much soul-searching.

Wouldn't it be tragic to take a hard line and then discover, after many young people have walked out the back door, that the issue wasn't really morally significant after all? That it was a gnat instead of a camel? It has happened—and is happening.

Young people may legitimately choose at times not to conform to the expectations of an older generation—even though they know their actions will be frowned on. However, they must ask themselves whether the issue is sufficiently important to risk the potential alienation.

The younger generation shouldn't be forever locked into the old way of doing things. On the other hand, when they choose to abandon tradition, they need to examine their decision seriously to ensure that they aren't losing something crucial.

Increasingly the church is becoming diverse. The ethnic mix, the mix of young and old, the mix of highly educated and less educated, the mix of rich and poor mean that we need tolerance and understanding as never before.

We mustn't let go of what really counts. But we must make sure it really *does* count before we risk offending others by insisting on preserving it. It's too easy for us to assume that *our* culture and *our* way of doing things is the best.

We need to try to distinguish between cultural claims and moral claims. Unfortunately, history doesn't offer much hope in that respect. Culture and morality become so intertwined in our minds that separating them is all but impossible. But we must separate them if we are to retain credibility.

If in our striving to do what is best we make mistakes—and we undoubtedly will—let it be on the side of too much tolerance rather than too much forced conformity.

Let it be on the side of taking too much time seeking to understand the thinking of others rather than too much time trying to drag them into line.

We become more understanding when we try to look from another person's perspective. We become more Christlike when we try to walk in another person's shoes—whatever style or color they may be.

And the best way to avoid seeing our names written in the dust is to drop the stones from our hands.

RELATING TO CHRIST'S BRIDE

Effective Dissent

From time to time in the church many of us see something that doesn't meet our approval and about which we feel we must protest. But we often fail to realize just how much our approach can influence whether our comments will be taken seriously.

Obviously, church leaders can't implement every suggestion that comes to them. But there are approaches by which we can enhance the likelihood of them doing so.

1. We should avoid prefacing our letters with pronouncements that the church is in utter apostasy, that the leader to whom we're writing is an infiltrator from some group antagonistic to Adventism, or that the leader doesn't care how we feel.

Undoubtedly, the church has its problems; it isn't what it should be. And, like Elijah, we may sometimes feel that we alone haven't bowed the knee to Baal. But even during Elijah's time things were 7,000 times better than he perceived them to be (1 Kings 19:18).

All would-be reformers must be as "wise as serpents, and harmless as doves" (Matthew 10:16). They also must never forget that a drop of honey catches more flies than a gallon of gall. We needn't be flatterers; but neither can we afford to be belligerent.

2. We need to make our point quickly. If we want to write a book on the problem, that's fine. We can send it along as a support document. But our letter needs to say in as few words as possible just what our concern is and how it can be remedied.

Church leaders are busy. Therefore, we should state our case completely but succinctly. We should support it with the strongest two or three quotations related to the issue—but not expect someone to read through pages and pages of quotations.

3. If a letter is written neatly, it will have more impact. No matter how objective and unbiased a church leader may try to be, he or she inevitably will respond more favorably to a tidy page for which the words have been carefully chosen and all the polishing done in earlier drafts.

A quality idea deserves a quality package. So if we really have a burden about the topic and want to have our comments make their optimum impact, it would be a worthwhile investment to type the letter or to pay to have it typed. And certainly it would be advantageous to have a few friends or family members serve as editors to correct flaws in the argument as well as in the grammar and spelling.

This isn't to say that church leaders listen only to people who send them model letters. But we must keep in mind that they may receive many letters both pro and con. Therefore, our comments are actually competing for credibility.

4. Finally, we must let church leaders know that we recognize that they must make difficult decisions and that the issues may be more complex than we realize. We should let them know that we're praying for them and that, whatever decision they ultimately make, they'll still have our goodwill. They need to know that even though we may oppose something they do, we're a loyal opposition.

These four suggestions are applicable only in situations in which we really want to see a situation changed and in which we truly want to be Christlike in our dealings.

If, on the other hand, we just want to let leaders know how much we despise them for being so blind as not to see things exactly as we do, and if we just want to put people down, then the options for insult and invective are almost limitless.

RELATING TO CHRIST'S BRIDE

Giving and Getting

One might easily get the impression from reading mission stories that missions are a one-way street—that missionaries go everywhere helping those less fortunate, while getting nothing in return.

In reality, however, it's not all giving. There's getting as well. And we mustn't underestimate the importance of the recipients' contribution to our understanding of what Christianity should be.

Inevitably, religion and culture become so intermingled that it's difficult to tell where one ends and the other begins. To a degree—too great a degree at times—Christian missionaries have been exporters of Western culture.

In the name of Christianity we've made demands of non-Western converts that aren't called for by Scripture. This is highly unfortunate. But, I'm happy to say, it isn't as widespread as it once was. And this is part of the getting.

The very fact that missionaries are uprooted from their culture and thrust into a culture that's radically different forces them to reassess many of their own values. Because of this process, and because of the sheer number of Christians who now reside in non-Western countries, the Christian church itself has had to do a lot of reassessing.

When I was 19 years old, I participated in the church's student missionary program. I took a break from study to serve as a volunteer in a non-Western country.

I had grown up on a small farm in rural America and had traveled relatively little prior to my mission experience. Thus I learned far more than I was ever able to impart to my students.

That year was the high point of my spiritual experience. I had no person my own age and from my own culture and language group with whom to associate. So, while I was extremely busy with my teaching, during what free time I had I was to a great degree on my own.

I'd always been so caught up in social activities that I'd scarcely had time to think about spiritual things. Now I suddenly had time to study, pray, reflect, and read the biographies of such great Christians as Albert Schweitzer and C. S. Lewis and George Mueller. Many issues sorted themselves out in my mind that year.

My values changed dramatically. I'd determined to enter as fully as possible into the experience of my host country. Thus I ate in the dining hall with my students. And I refused to allow myself the luxuries that my money could buy but that my students couldn't afford.

I found the food monotonous and unsatisfying. But I refused to use personal funds to provide greater variety for myself. Further, it wasn't really necessary. We were getting proper nutrition. Only my pampered palate was suffering.

What really made me stop and think, however, was a group of people from a nearby village. Every morning at dawn they lined up near the back door of the school kitchen, waiting for the scraps of the food I detested. Ostensibly they were taking it home to their pigs (they have their pride, you know). But many a time I saw them slyly slipping morsels from their buckets into their mouths.

While I was daily watching such scenes, I was receiving the student newspaper from the college I had attended the year before. The newspaper featured a running debate over whether the college should construct a piece of ornamental architecture (at a cost of $200,000, I believe it was) that would be symbolic of some school tradition. I was enraged by the debate.

Several years later when I took a group of young volunteers to another non-Western country to construct an addition on a small hospital, I noticed how even three weeks there had changed their outlook. And I've met few people who've served as either short-term or long-term missionaries who haven't come home with a totally different set of priorities and values.

And those values aren't *just* culturally related. The questions non-Western converts to Christianity have asked and are asking mean that missionaries are forced to reassess their own perceptions of Christianity. If we're honest, we'll have to admit that Western Christianity has lost sight of many of the values that New Testament Christianity stood for. And in some of these areas the non-Western world is forcing us back to a more pure religion.

So Christian missions don't just give. They get. They get much. The missionaries' lives are enriched as a result of having lived in a different culture. But more than that, the Christian church itself is forced back to certain basics that have been ignored for too long.

For this, we owe a debt of gratitude to the recipients of our message. They've proved what the wise man said: "He who refreshes others will himself be refreshed" (Proverbs 11:25, NIV).

RELATING TO CHRIST'S BRIDE

Here to Stay

During the past five decades at least three changes have taken place in society that have dramatically affected, and will continue to affect, the Seventh-day Adventist Church.

First, students in both Adventist and public schools have been taught to analyze and question everything. Nothing is exempt. No assumptions are safe from scrutiny.

Second, the social convulsion of the 1960s and 1970s has, for the most part, left two generations with a mind-set that's totally different from the mind-set of earlier generations.

The *group* has taken a back seat to the *individual.* The search for an abstract "textbook" truth has given way to a quest for personal fulfillment. Function has become the ultimate test: What does going to church do for me? Why should I remain married if I feel I'm getting nothing from it? How does believing in the Sabbath affect my everyday life? In short, what's in it for me?

Third, people 55 years of age and younger have, for the most part, been strongly influenced by television. Thus, they expect to receive everything in a prepackaged, fast-moving, action-packed form.

Realistically, we must face the fact that these changes are here to stay. Things will never return to what they once were. And we wouldn't necessarily want them to—because the changes, though unsettling in many ways, aren't all bad.

After all, the goal of education *is* to teach the youth to be "thinkers, and not mere reflectors of other men's thought" (Ellen White, *Education,* p. 17). Religion *should* be relevant to the basics of living. And why shouldn't we as a church cash in on what television producers have learned about human motivation?

Thus, in the final analysis, we have three options before us: We can decry the changes. We can try to ignore the changes. Or we can acknowledge the changes and do what we can to make the church relevant to an ever-expanding group that currently is dwelling on the fringes in alarmingly large numbers—not to mention the equally large group that has slipped out the church's back door already.

And this group isn't made up only of teenagers. It includes many people with grown children. So what do we need?

We don't need a new theology. But we do need to rethink our theology so we can present old truths in a way that makes them more relevant to everyday life.

We don't need to turn our worship services into Hollywood productions. But we do need to make our services more interesting, varied, and active. We need to include as many participants as possible. We need to generate a greater sense of fellowship and Christian community.

We don't need to make younger people the sole focus as we seek to structure the church service for optimum impact. But we do need to recognize that young people have been and are being given little more than token consideration in far too many congregations.

We don't need to change simply for the sake of change. But we do need to recognize that to remain viable, the church, like any corporate structure, must make certain adjustments to keep pace with the times.

We don't need to give up any major truth we hold. But we do need to reassess a host of procedural traditions that have been elevated to the level of spiritual truths in the minds of many.

Since it began 2,000 years ago, the Christian church has done amazingly well in meeting the varied needs of different times and places. But never have society's and individual thought patterns changed with such speed as has happened in recent decades.

Understandably, such rapid change is disconcerting for many older people and disorienting for many younger ones. But if we seek together to understand what has happened and is happening, and if after having assessed the changes we hold on to that which is good, our church will be far more effective in getting on with the tasks God has given it to do.

RELATING TO CHRIST'S BRIDE

Inoculated

Smallpox, one of the world's most dreaded plagues until 1977 (the year of the last known naturally occurring case—in 1980 the World Health Organization declared it eradicated), fell victim to a process known as inoculation (or immunization).

By 1978 active smallpox virus existed in only 11 laboratories around the world, and plans called for that number to be reduced to four. Inoculation had worked well.

Inoculation is the introduction into the system of some substance—sometimes an impotent form of the virus itself—that makes the body develop an immunity to the real thing if and when it's encountered.

Today one of the biggest dangers facing Christianity in general and Adventism in particular is that it also will fall victim to inoculation.

The gospel should be contagious. The Jewish leaders during and immediately after the time of Christ viewed its spread as an epidemic. By the end of the first century it had gone to the then-known world.

Unlike the laboratories that deal with the smallpox virus, the church, the repository of truth, is to do all within its power to make the contagion of God's love spread. That's the reason for its existence. However, the church also has the power to inoculate, virtually guaranteeing that people will never experience the gospel in its true beauty.

People who are exposed to a form of Christianity that bases its beliefs more on human teachings than on the Word of God are apt to be disillusioned. If that's what Christianity is all about, they might as well listen to anyone else's philosophies.

If there's an imbalance in emphasis on what God has done for us and what God can and will do in us and through us, people can easily develop the idea that God is indifferent to sin or, conversely, that He's an unreasonable taskmaster in what He expects of His followers. Either weakens the gospel's power.

When the pulpit is used merely to expound the latest findings of psychology or to provide political commentary, the gospel is weakened, for people could gain the same information by subscribing to a good magazine or joining a professional organization or political party. While such matters may be of significance to the Christian, they don't provide the unique contribution that the gospel alone can give.

Should people come to the church expecting to find love but instead find ill feelings, grudges, backbiting, and dissension, they may want no part of it. If they begin to feel that that's what Christianity is all about, they'll continue to look elsewhere.

Learning to inoculate against smallpox was a great scientific breakthrough. The fact that we often so effectively inoculate against true Christianity is a tragedy.

RELATING TO CHRIST'S BRIDE

Judging the Sheepfolds

When I was an editor, I edited literally hundreds of stories about conversions to the Seventh-day Adventist Church. The stories were usually inspiring. But they often contained an element that left me uncomfortable.

So I ask now the question I wrestled with then: Is it really necessary to name the denomination from which a convert to Adventism has come? Must we identify which religious group failed to spiritually fulfill the person concerned?

Must we specify which denomination persecuted Adventists who were trying to share their faith in an area previously unentered by our church? Is anything gained by pointing to the shortcomings of specific groups of fellow believers in Christ?

A few years ago I had the unpleasant experience of facing this issue from the receiving end. One of my fellow editors happened upon an Australian religious journal containing an article about a Seventh-day Adventist minister who'd left the church to become a pastor in another denomination.

The title of the article suggested that his departure from Adventism was like "leaving a darkened room." Needless to say, the ex-Adventist's comments were less than complimentary. Judging by what he had to say, our church is a spiritual wasteland. I'm certain that what he said is exactly what he felt. However, his perceptions didn't mesh with mine. In fact, I was rather upset to see my church caricatured in that manner in another denomination's journal.

In the same way, a good many Baptists, Lutherans, Catholics, or you name it wouldn't recognize themselves in the "spiritual wasteland" descriptions sometimes given them. Many in those communions would say that the perceptions of the defectors are incorrect—which is what I said about the comments of the former Adventist minister.

With this in mind, when I was an editor I followed a policy of not specifying the name of the religious organization from which new Adventists may have come—be it a Christian denomination or a non-Christian belief system. Rarely does such information add anything essential to the story. And members of the faith so named might well be justified in feeling that Adventists are putting down their faith. Naming others can easily contribute to an Adventist superiority complex as well.

Thus our aim (although mistakes slipped through) was simply to say that before becoming an Adventist, the person was a member of "another Christian denomination" or of "a non-Christian faith." Nothing more. And I wish a similar policy were universally advocated for all oral and written presentations.

Some time ago I listened to a prominent church leader who was strongly promoting the approach I've just outlined. He told how early in his ministry this attitude caused his orthodoxy to be questioned. The body to which he was responsible called him in and asked just exactly what he did believe.

"I recognize every agency that lifts up Christ before men and women as a part of the divine plan for evangelization of the world," he said, "and I hold in high esteem the Christian men and women in other communions who are engaged in winning souls to Christ."

"It's worse than we even thought!" said one of the men carrying out the inquiry.

But this man didn't realize that the young minister wasn't speaking his own words. He was reiterating the General Conference *Working Policy,* which clearly outlines the attitude Adventists should have toward other religious organizations.

If we believe what our working policy states, we should be cautious in using even such phrases as "brought to Christ" and "became a Christian." Having people join the Seventh-day Adventist Church isn't necessarily synonymous with coming to Christ. Many were solid Christians for years before becoming Adventists.

Perhaps in detailing stories of people's spiritual pilgrimages we should keep two texts in mind: "Other sheep I have, which are not of this fold" (John 10:16) and "Whatsoever ye would that men should do to you, do ye even so to them" (Matthew 7:12).

RELATING TO CHRIST'S BRIDE

Just Call Me Jim

During the years I worked as an editor, never a week went by without my receiving at least one letter from someone lamenting that things weren't what they used to be.

And they were right. The church has changed. The ministers have changed. Their sermons have changed. Their emphasis has changed. Adventist institutions have changed. Even the way we address each other has changed.

And speaking of how we address each other, why don't we say "Brother" and "Sister" as we did in the good old days before all this change set in?

Now, let me make it absolutely clear to those who favor the use of such terms as "Brother" and "Sister" that I'm 100 percent on your side. And let me make it absolutely clear to those who prefer not to use such terms that I'm 100 percent on your side, too. But how can I take both positions? Isn't that playing politics? duplicity?

Let's go back 100 years to when the Adventist Church was still in its infancy. It was customary in most social situations to refer to people by their surnames, prefaced by a title. Rarely were people referred to by first names. And almost never would a younger person refer to an older person by a first name.

But church members had a sense of oneness, a sense of family, a sense of intimacy that needed to be expressed in some manner. So Adventists adopted the already-common Christian practice of using "Brother" and "Sister" with the surname in place of "Mr.," "Mrs.," "Miss," or "Ms" (which didn't even exist back then).

Not only did this help them feel closer to each other by giving them a set of titles for fellow church members different from those they used for nonmembers; it also was a constant reminder of a major theological truth: the Bible tells us that God is our Father, Christ is our Brother, and therefore we're all brothers and sisters and thus equal before God.

This is the context in which many older Adventists today view "Brother" and "Sister." For them these terms have great meaning. And this is why I say I support them 100 percent. But now to the other side.

In the years that have elapsed since our church was founded, society has changed dramatically. Most people 50 years of age and younger use titles only when they feel a sense of distance from another person. We live in the era of first names. And after all, isn't the first name sometimes even referred to as the "Christian name"?

Few under-50s would feel that referring to fellow church member Ginger Smith as "Sister Smith" is as intimate as simply calling her "Ginger." In today's society there's a tremendous need to belong and be accepted. And in the minds of most younger Adventists, first names indicate closeness; titles indicate an arm's-length relationship.

Although younger Adventists wouldn't deny the theology behind "Brother" and "Sister," most would probably feel that the theological benefit of using such terms isn't sufficient compensation for the lost sense of intimacy that titles create.

Furthermore, because it's almost exclusively older Adventists who use such titles, the younger Adventists have come to view their use as old-fashioned. Thus, in situations in which they definitely feel a title is necessary, they inevitably prefer to use the more universal "Mr.," "Mrs.," "Miss," or "Ms." It just comes more naturally. I fully appreciate their viewpoint on this topic. That's why I can also say that I agree with them 100 percent.

Maybe there are parallels here to the kind of situation the apostle Paul addressed in Romans 14 concerning meat that had been offered to idols. Those who choose to use such titles are doing it to show respect to their fellow Adventists, to show their acceptance of them, and to show their brotherhood and sisterhood with them.

On the other hand, those who choose not to use such titles haven't rejected the theology of God as Father and Christ as Brother. They simply feel that close relationships, family relationships, are more meaningful when not encumbered by titles.

RELATING TO CHRIST'S BRIDE

Learning to Fly

During the past three or four decades the Seventh-day Adventist Church in the Western world has changed dramatically. Today we see in the church a far broader range of ideas and behavior than would once have been tolerated. But not everyone feels comfortable with the concept of tolerance.

At the extremes, one group in our church looks to the past and wishes we could recapture a spiritual quality they feel we have lost. The other group looks to the future and longs for something they feel hasn't yet existed. One group looks for more guidelines and clearer definitions. The other group advocates focusing on principles and leaving most final decisions to the individual.

One group rejoices when "the trumpet is given a certain sound." The other group is heartened when someone admits that we don't have all the answers.

One group emphasizes traditional evangelism, with its focus on prophecy and its emphasis on propositional truth. The other group emphasizes the need to love other people into a relationship with Christ.

Unfortunately, each group is leery of the other. Each tends to view the other as the cause for the church's current relative lack of progress. But are these perceptions correct?

I believe that until we learn to appreciate the strengths and weaknesses of both approaches, the work of the church is going to suffer. As a colleague of mine puts it: "In order to fly, a bird needs a right wing, a left wing, and a good body between." The same applies to the church.

The church needs a group of people who constantly question the wisdom of change, who are deeply concerned lest we lose sight of our church's original mission.

And the church equally needs a group who ever push us on to new frontiers, who clamor for greater consistency, who force us to reevaluate our mission, who ensure that we're speaking to and meeting the needs of people in our world today.

One group safeguards us from going off on a tangent. The other safeguards us from slipping into a rut. Each type of thinking has its merits.

For example, the more a message is presented in black-and-white terms, the more likely it is to attract converts. By contrast, tolerance makes great friends, but it doesn't make people sense that they must change or risk damnation.

Openness creates a healthy environment for discussion and the exchange of ideas, but certainty gets people into the baptismal font. Certainty also gets them into tithing, giving generous offerings, and working long hours for the church.

Both aspects are important, though, and we need to keep the long term in mind as well as the short term. Subsequent generations of Adventists need room to forge their own faith. And unless they find a tolerant environment for their own spiritual quest, they'll simply drop out.

So when I hear people on the left murmuring about the need to muzzle the right, I become a champion of the right. And when those on the right want to muzzle—or even disfranchise—the left, I champion the left.

Rather than taking the narrow-minded position that we would be better off if we eliminated "the opposition," we need to recognize that even though people with a differing view may cause us discomfort, they play a vital role in keeping the church vibrant and on course.

Only when the right wing and the left wing both exist, only when they both recognize their need to stay firmly attached to the body, only when they allow the love of God to soften their hearts and make them sensitive to others, will our church ever soar to the heights that God intended for it.

RELATING TO CHRIST'S BRIDE

Memorable Experiences

One of the most memorable sermons I heard as a teenager was based on an amazing story the speaker had read in a religious journal a few months before. The story, if true, was significant indeed.

As he told it, a group of scientists at the NASA installation at Greenbelt, Maryland, were doing some computerized astronomical calculations to determine the exact position of the heavenly bodies for centuries back into the past so they could plot them for centuries into the future.

As the calculations moved further and further back through time, the computer suddenly stopped. A signal came on indicating that something was incorrect. The results weren't consistent with the standard calculations against which the computer was comparing its own findings. Either the computer calculations were wrong, or the information being fed into it was inaccurate.

The scientists checked and rechecked. The information was correct. The computer was functioning perfectly. But they had a problem: A day was missing. How could it be?

Then one of the men remembered something he had heard in Sunday school years before—about Joshua commanding the sun to stand still. They brought a Bible, and there it was: "So the sun stood still in the midst of heaven, and hasted not to go down about a whole day" (Joshua 10:13).

Thinking they had the answer, they went back to their computer. But, alas, they discovered that they had accounted for only 23 hours and 20 minutes. No worry. The Bible had said that it was "about a whole day." Perhaps that was close enough.

Then someone remembered another Sunday school story—about

Hezekiah asking that the sun's shadow move back 10 degrees (2 Kings 20:8-10).

There it was! Ten degrees. The missing 40 minutes exactly! The Bible had provided the answer for a question that had baffled America's best scientific minds using the most sophisticated computer technology.

It was an impressive basis for a sermon—except for one thing. Only the night before I had read an article in an Adventist magazine—that had arrived only a few days earlier—in which the entire story was exposed as a fraud. It never happened—even though the story writer had cited specific names and places.

From the body language of various people in the congregation, and from a few panicky whispers that passed between husbands and wives when the speaker started telling the story, I knew that I wasn't the only one to have read the disclaimer article.

I also knew that the speaker subscribed to the magazine in which I had read the disclaimer. And I wondered what he would think when he read it—probably during his Sabbath afternoon reading that very day!

That memorable sermon was preached about 30 years ago. But, unfortunately, the story has resurfaced periodically since. And it's still making the rounds in some Adventist churches. But—and I repeat—it is not true.

As a group, Adventists are too ready to grant credence to sensational stories—particularly if they seem to go along with beliefs we hold strongly. But our faith shouldn't require such evidences. In fact, such dramatic evidences, if available, would all but make faith unnecessary.

No doubt the story's author was well-intentioned. The writer may have so wanted skeptics to believe in the Bible that he or she decided that the ends justified the means. But do they?

For me, the story was memorable because of the irony created by the context in which it was presented. No real harm was done.

But for the skeptics who hear it—and many other stories like it—it will also be memorable, but in a far more negative way. Nothing so solidifies skeptics in their skepticism, and nothing is so memorable to skeptics, as catching Christians red-handed in perpetrating a fraud.

Let's be on guard against giving them that kind of memory.

Needed: A Statute of Limitation

In the legal world the passage of time is often considered significant. Statutes of limitation prohibit prosecution after a specified time lapse. While such legal provisions may have their negative features, they serve as a safeguard for the accused.

As Christians we don't function in a manner analogous to the legal system. Nevertheless, the statute-of-limitation principle, the concern to safeguard the accused, is one we need to implement far more frequently than we do.

Even when a person is unquestionably guilty of behavior that we consider morally or ethically unacceptable (and more so when guilt remains unproven), we should not parade that lapse before the church public in perpetuity. We need to forgive and forget.

For a brief period I had the pleasure of working closely with a Christian gentleman as nearly "representative" as I've met. His loyalty and dedication to Christ and the church were admirable. He displayed a rare sensitivity and concern for others. It was easy to see why he held a significant church office. So you can imagine my surprise when I discovered that not many years before he'd served time in prison.

Although he'd been reared an Adventist and was active in the church, he had succumbed to an embezzlement scheme. Once involved, he found it impossible to get out without exposing the other participants. As he was wrestling with what course of action to take, the scheme was exposed. He pleaded guilty, admitted his sense of relief at being caught, and served his sentence.

Fortunately, because his fellow church members believed in both God's forgiveness and His power to transform, they, in effect, observed a statute of limitation. Never did I hear even one member bring up the man's past. Only when I happened to visit another city many miles away did someone tell me the story.

In contrast, I served as assistant pastor in a church where one of the members had been a denominational employee holding an important position. Many years before, marital infidelity had led to his dismissal. Even though he had repented, been rebaptized, was a loyal supporter of the church in every way, and lived a life that none could fault, the suggestion of his name as a possible Sabbath school teacher raised many an eyebrow.

Unfortunately, certain members of the congregation didn't observe a statute of limitation. And by failing to do so, they were denying God's willingness to forgive and transform.

It's ironic that we elevate almost to celebrity status those people who were in the pit of human degradation before coming to know Christ. To our credit, we generally fail to see the terrible stains of the past that now are covered by Christ's robe of righteousness.

But let a person already wearing that robe become tarnished, and we too often develop vision so sensitive that it can penetrate even divine coverings and detect stains of many years gone by.

As Christians we shouldn't cease to call sin by its right name. But we should recognize that the only person qualified to do so is the one equally conversant with grace.

While it's impossible to specify the time lapse necessary for rehabilitation after a spiritual fall and genuine repentance, surely it isn't as well-nigh eternal as we've often implied by our actions. Less than eight weeks after denial of his Master, Peter was the featured speaker at the Pentecost revival series. How many years would have had to elapse before the early church would have begun to ignore the past of the woman taken in adultery?

In dealing with erring humanity, we must never lose sight of the awfulness of sin. More important, though, we must never forget that God loves all sinners, and God saves repentant sinners.

There's a God in heaven who can forgive all manner of sin and then hide it in the depths of the ocean. The real question is Can we?

RELATING TO CHRIST'S BRIDE

One Man's View

Most of us as Adventists love to see Adventists mentioned in the media. Provided the comments are favorable, that is.

Actually, during my years of editing Adventist news for Adventist publications, I discovered that many of the news items didn't focus primarily on an Adventist-sponsored event, but on the fact that some newspaper or television station gave extensive and positive coverage to the event.

However, not all media coverage of Adventists and Adventist events is positive. And while negative comment may not be as pleasing to our eyes and ears, it may in the long run be more instructive.

Since most Adventists aren't major connoisseurs of the performing arts, the name Bob Ellis may not ring a bell—particularly to those who don't live in Australia, where he lives. Bob Ellis is a controversial Australian "playwright, lyricist, movie writer and director, television and film critic, orator, and night club comic," as the host of an Australian radio interview show described him a few years ago. And Bob Ellis grew up a Seventh-day Adventist.

As you no doubt have guessed, he is no longer an Adventist. But he was sufficiently influenced by Adventism—at least as it was portrayed to him—that he credits it with having had a major influence on his life. And that influence, as far as he is concerned, was less than positive.

Being an Adventist "meant that I grew up with a nose-pressed-to-the-glass attitude, because we were forbidden to do a lot of things," he said during a radio interview.

Bob Ellis didn't have a positive attitude toward Adventism even as a child. At school he often claimed to be a member of the Salvation Army to avoid the "shame" of admitting he was an Adventist. At the same time, he says he felt "self-righteous because I knew we were right."

But being "right" wasn't enough to make his religion satisfying. And as soon as possible, he escaped it. But he still reminisces publicly and frequently about the attitude toward life that he gained from his Adventist experience.

When I read a couple of articles about Bob Ellis and heard him interviewed, my first reaction to his comments about Adventists was to say, "Now, wait a minute! You're mistaken! That's not what Adventists are like. You're badly misrepresenting us. We're not as negative as you make us appear. After all, I've been an Adventist a lot longer than you, and I think it's a dynamic and positive religion. Don't you caricature my beliefs like that!"

Then I began to think about it. Why should I assume that this man, earthy and worldly-wise though he might be, is not describing the whole experience *exactly* as he perceived it? And more frightening still, is it possible that his perceptions were right—at least in the contacts that he had?

Certainly the majority of Adventists don't have the attitudes he describes. Certainly the majority of Adventists don't live a life of don'ts. But unfortunately, some of us haven't been as effective in showing the beauty of our religion as we should have been. Some of us have dwelt on the negative far too much.

We've talked too much about the things we've had to give up rather than about how much we're getting in return. We've made it sound as if life on this earth is merely to be endured and that only in the next life will we have real pleasure. In reality, life is to be lived to the full both here and now and in the eternal realm.

Yes, Bob Ellis doesn't think much of Adventism. And if it's because he's closed-minded, biased, unperceptive, or plain dishonest, it's most unfortunate. But if it's because the Adventists he met truly were everything he describes them to be, it's a tragedy. And we need to see that it isn't repeated.

Repeating the Past

The makeup of the Jewish "church" in the time of Jesus may have significance for the Adventist Church in the early twenty-first century. Let's look just briefly at the various groups Christ would have encountered.

First, there were the Pharisees. The origin of this group is somewhat obscure, but it seems their reason for being was closely connected with concern over the inroads of Greek thought into their religion. They felt it was crucial to restore Judaism's orthodoxy—"the truth"—in face of what they saw as totally unacceptable compromises in both theology and behavior.

Judaism was not just another religion. It was *the* religion. And the Pharisees were determined that it should never lose its uniqueness. While Jews had to exist in the world, the Pharisees wanted to safeguard them against becoming corrupted by the world. Therefore, they advocated strict adherence to the Torah and all the traditions that had grown up around it—whether they were God-given or not. Life for them was black-and-white. Shades of gray didn't exist.

Pharisees enjoyed nothing more than winning a theological debate against a non-Pharisee. And they were constantly on the lookout for a chance to discredit as heretics those who didn't agree completely with their point of view. Truth for them came in the form of rules and statements that were easily defined and concrete.

The Pharisees acknowledged that the church hierarchy was God-ordained, but they sought to influence it toward their point of view. In fact, they were a highly effective lobby group that made an impact quite disproportionate to their numbers, which were relatively limited.

Despite their strictness, the Pharisees were almost liberal compared to a second group—the Essenes. This group demanded an almost monastic existence, choosing to separate themselves from their fellow Jews, whom they considered apostate, and from the world in general, which they viewed as totally evil.

The Essenes' radical lifestyle and their emphasis on dress, diet, and separateness meant that their numbers were even more limited than the Pharisees. However, this merely added to their conviction that they alone were the true representatives of Judaism and Jehovah.

But Judaism had its liberal contingent, too. The Sadducees were highly educated "modernists" who sought to make their religion acceptable to the world of Greek thought. Rational, and to a great degree secular, they were Judaism's "demythologizers." Unlike the Pharisees, who usually kept their distance from politics, the Sadducees virtually constituted a political party. They were willing to rub shoulders with the world.

The issues at stake in the debate between these three groups were all but meaningless to those who were not highly educated and widely read in Jewish religious literature. However, the majority of the common people found greater affinity with the Pharisees than with the other two groups. The Essenes were too demanding, while the Sadducees were not sufficiently traditional. The latter were also suspect because of their reliance on secular knowledge.

Despite their many differences, however, common elements did exist between these three groups. Each group was concerned about real and legitimate issues. But ironically, each group was more interested in "truth" and proper behavior than in the way people should be treated.

Each group had all the answers. And, as "it is not the healthy who need a doctor, but the sick," each group found no use for The Answer when He came. As a result, it was another group—the outcasts, the group who would seem the least likely—who accepted the Messiah.

But why do I take time to write about things that happened so long ago? Because, as George Santayana once observed, "those who cannot remember the past are condemned to repeat it."

Self-conversing

I'm going to let you in on the details of an imaginary discussion I had recently.

You see, I like to talk to myself. For one thing, I always find myself an attentive listener. At times I'm even impressed by what I have to say. But more important, it gives me a chance to test some of my ideas in a true-to-life situation (albeit imaginary) before going public with them.

And, being in control of the input from both sides, I usually do a pretty good job of presenting my case. Rarely do I fail to win my point—even though the other side poses some pretty tough questions. But the other day something went awry.

I was pointing out to myself (somewhat arrogantly, I might add) the significance of the Seventh-day Adventist Church's not having become locked in by a creed. "In fact," I said, warming to my topic, "our denomination's pioneers rarely described our organization as a 'church.' They preferred to call it a 'movement.' "

I went on to contrast the Adventists' concept of "present truth" with the unbending dogmas of some other Christian bodies.

Obviously I was stating my case quite eloquently. And the questions coming back were of equally high caliber—though I fancy that I slightly had the upper hand.

"You say you see truth as an ongoing thing that unfolds with time?"

"Quite right," I replied. "That's why it's so crucial not to have our beliefs set in concrete. We need to allow for growth in understanding."

"Would you say that the same principle applies to experience? Should our experience be deeper today than it was, say, 10 years ago?"

"Certainly," I said, delighted at such astute questions. "We should be growing all the time. That's what the Christian life is all about."

"Obviously, if there's this constant growth, then people will be at different levels of development, depending on how fast they grow and how long they've been growing. Right?"

"Absolutely," I said with conviction (and not a little pride that my point was being perceived so well).

"Then, just how much have you developed spiritually in the past 10 years?"

"I think you're missing the point," I said, not liking the direction the discussion was suddenly taking. "You're turning this into legalism. You can't work your way to heaven. God never intended us to have a checklist religion."

"True. But shouldn't you be able to look at your life and say, 'I used to be a drunk in the gutter, but now I am, by God's grace, staying sober?'

"Shouldn't you be able to say, "I used to use profane language, but, thanks be to God, I no longer talk that way?'

"Shouldn't you be able to say, 'I used to eat too many sweets at the church potlucks, but over the years my knowledge of what's healthful has increased, and I now feel much more fit physically because God has helped me follow through on what I know to be right?' "

"Shouldn't you be able to say, 'I used to be highly insensitive to the needs of those less fortunate, but God has been helping me understand the self-centeredness of my approach'?"

"Well, yes, but . . ."

"My point is, if you're going to talk about a 'movement,' and if you're going to use such words as health 'reform,' then I would like to know just how much you personally have *moved* and *reformed* during the past few years, and just how much better life is for you every day because of it. Or is your Christian experience at the same level as—or even lower than—it was 10 years ago? And what good is a *belief* system that has flexibility if your *experience* never moves ahead?"

Fortunately, I suddenly remembered that I had an appointment, so I brought the conversation to a close. And none too soon, either. Because I don't like that kind of talk.

In fact, if another of my conversations with myself degenerates to that level, something may have to change.

RELATING TO CHRIST'S BRIDE

Silence the Trumpets?

Some years ago a radical thought somehow slipped past all the conventional thought-screening sentries that usually control what enters my mind. Yet no sooner had the thought slipped in than my mind-guards seized it, bound it, and threw it out.

A few months later the same thought sneaked in again. But not before I had a chance to interrogate it. And I didn't like its answers. Every time I asked it a question, it merely replied, "Well, what do *you* think?"

Despite valiant efforts on my part, the thought returns periodically. And I've noticed that without exception, it happens when I reflect on Matthew 6:1-4.

For a while I considered avoiding that passage altogether. But the words of 2 Timothy 3:16 kept ringing in my head—"All Scripture is . . . useful for teaching, rebuking, correcting and training in righteousness" (NIV).

So what does Matthew 6:1-4 say? In brief, it says: "Be careful not to do your 'acts of righteousness' before men. . . . When you give to the needy, do not announce it with trumpets. . . . Do not let your left hand know what your right hand is doing" (NIV).

"There's nothing radical about that," you say. "It's just a call to avoid pride and display."

True. But when the Bible lays down principles of personal behavior, don't they apply to groups, also?

Are groups immune to the foibles of individuals? Can a group become proud? Can a group smite itself on its collective breast and say, "Thank God that we're not like that *group* of publicans"? Can a group say, "Our *group* is better than your *group"?*

At the time the radical thought first appeared, I just happened to be preparing a presentation for about 150 church communication secretaries. In it I was suggesting ways to wring every bit of publicity out of every "act of righteousness" the Seventh-day Adventist Church does.

And the thought suddenly struck me: Should I instead be teaching them how to do good deeds *secretly,* so that no one will know who it was who did them?

"Don't be stupid," you say. "If we didn't use the media to attract people's attention, we wouldn't see a fraction of the conversions we now have. We wouldn't have nearly as much goodwill. Besides, every other religious group uses media publicity to build name recognition and credibility."

I know. I've used the same words when I've argued with the radical thought. But let me suggest an altogether different scenario.

Suppose we as Adventists determine *not* to let our "acts of righteousness" become public. Suppose that, when the Pathfinders go down to tidy up the lawn of an old couple who've been ill, they don't reveal their identity. When asked who they are, they simply say, "Just a group of Christian young people who care."

Suppose disaster strikes, and the conference van rolls up, loaded with blankets and sandwiches and hot drinks—*without* the name, address, and phone number on the side of the van. When people ask who's providing this wonderful humanitarian service, the Adventist volunteers simply say, "Just a group of Christians who care."

Suppose we inundate the community with hundreds of deeds of kindness and helpfulness, both large and small. But whenever onlookers or those who've been helped ask who's doing it, we reply, "Just a group of Christians who care."

My guess is that before long the newspaper and radio and TV stations would have reporters out trying to find out the identity of this "group of Christians who care."

I'm not saying that this hypothetical outline *would* be a good idea. It might be the formula for disaster. (Of course, Christianity has never been a formula for "success.") But it can't hurt to at least ask, as the radical thought always does to me, "Well, what do *you* think about it?"